THE FRESHWATER TACKLEBOX

John Merwin

B. Mitchell

A FRIEDMAN GROUP BOOK

Copyright ©1992 by Michael Friedman Publishing Group, Inc.

ISBN 0-88665-981-7

THE FRESHWATER TACKLEBOX
was prepared and produced by
Michael Friedman Publishing Group, Inc.
15 West 26th Street
New York, New York 10010
for SMITHBOOKS LTD.
113 Merton Street
Toronto, Ontario
M4S 1A8

Editor: Elizabeth Viscott Sullivan
Art Director: Jeff Batzli
Designer: Bob Michaels
Photography Researcher: Daniella Jo Nilva

Typeset by The Typecrafters Inc.
Color separation by Scantrans Pte. Ltd.
Printed and bound in Hong Kong by Leefung-Asco Printers Ltd.

Contents

INTRODUCTION

A modern freshwater tackle shop with a full complement of gear inevitably looks like the spare-parts center at NASA to the uninitiated. I often feel sorry for the novice angler who comes in the door and innocently tries to buy a rod or reel from the several hundred different models on the racks and shelves. Sometimes a salesperson is genuinely helpful in these situations, but then again, sometimes he or she is not. In either case, this book will help you select equipment that will meet your freshwater-fishing needs.

The Freshwater Tacklebox reviews, chapter-by-chapter, every essential component of freshwater-fishing tackle and is designed to help your fishing no matter where you might fish. Many veteran anglers often write about fishing in ways that only other veteran anglers can understand. While there are numerous tips that should be of value to experienced anglers, *The Freshwater Tacklebox* assumes no prior knowledge of fishing on the reader's part. With the help of this book, virtually anyone can select the right tackle and start fishing almost immediately. You'll

have an outfit that will actually work—instead of one that ends in a tangled, frustrating mess because it wasn't properly put together or its components weren't correctly matched.

Spin-casting, spinning, bait-casting, and fly-fishing tackle all have their particular adherents; consequently this book devotes several chapters to each one. I suggest, though, that you read *all* the chapters, even though some may not cover your favorite method, because much of the information therein will still be pertinent. The basic concepts of choosing a spinning rod, for example, also apply to many other types of rods, so reading the whole book will give you a complete picture before you head for your local tackle shop, or order equipment from a catalog.

The object of this exercise, of course, is catching fish, so I've also included some notes on the most popular game fishes—bass, trout, and others—to give you a basic idea of where and how to catch them. You'll need to assemble a balanced fishing outfit to do this, however, and the basis of *The Freshwater Tacklebox* is to help you do just that.

PART I
REELS

Although some traditions of freshwater angling extend back thousands of years, fishing reels are a relatively recent development. The oldest technique was simply to tie the fishing line directly to the tip of whatever rod was being used. This method limited the length of one's cast and the size of the fish that one could catch since it was impossible to play fish by releasing line and then reeling it back. Primitive brass "winches," as early reels were called, were in limited supply by the late 1600s, but it wasn't until the nineteenth-century industrial revolution in western Europe and North America that a broad variety of fishing reels came into widespread use.

Of the four modern reel types commonly used in freshwater fishing, bait-casting reels are the oldest and date back to the early design work of a few Kentucky watchmakers in the 1820s. Before the American Civil War, there was little physical difference between fly and other reel types. The modern ventilated spool fly reel did not emerge until 1874. Some early spinning reels were in limited production between 1905 and 1940, but were unpopular because the lines available at that time didn't work well on reels of this design. The development of monofilament nylon fishing line during World War II finally allowed spinning reels to become the most widely used freshwater tackle. Push-button, closed-face reels—now called spin-casting reels—were an outgrowth of spinning's development.

All of these reel types are described in detail in this section. Here's something to keep in mind that pertains to all of them: When choosing a reel, buy the best one you can afford. As with other types of tackle, a top-quality reel will inevitably provide longer and better service than a cheaper product. Quality tackle is always a good investment, regardless of your experience or skill.

Often I have thought how wonderful it would be to go fishing everywhere— in lakes and streams, in rivers, in the mountains, and on the seas.

—Zane Grey

Chapter 1
Spin-casting Reels

For easy operation, it's tough to beat a spin-casting reel. These reels require the least dexterity in casting of any possible combination and are obvious choices for most beginning freshwater anglers. Experienced anglers, too, may find these reels useful at times. The simple operation of these reels can be a big plus in situations such as fishing after dark with light lures for bass and walleyes.

Spin-casting reels are usually quite compact, with a removable, cone-shaped cover over the reel spool at the forward end of a small reel body and handle assembly. There is an elongated, flat piece of metal at the bottom, which is the reel foot. This foot slips into the rod's reelseat where it is secured by a screw-locking clamp. At the top rear of the reel body is a large button, the purpose of which is to hold and then release line for casting.

Like most other reels, spin-casting reels come with manufacturer's instructions for maintenance and use. Always read all instructions before using any new equipment. Directions are generally given for the right-handed angler, and are written as such in this book as well. Left-handed anglers, in most cases, should do the opposite.

The reel mounts on a spin-casting- or bait-casting-style rod (see Chapter 6) with its distinctive trigger-type reelseat. When correctly mounted, a spin-casting reel will be on top of the rod with its handle on the right side. Push and release the button on the top of the reel to free the line, then string the line through the rod guides and rod tip, being careful not

Courtesy Zebco Corporation

to miss any of the guides. Then use a Trilene Knot (page 123) to attach a snap swivel (page 121) to the line. For practice casting, use a hookless practice plug, sold in many tackle stores and catalogs; a ¼-ounce (7-g) version should be fine for most light- and medium-weight reels.

Casting is simple. Grip the rod handle comfortably in your right hand with your index finger around the trigger portion of the rod grip and your thumb resting to the left side of the reel. The trigger-grip helps support the rod during your casting motion. Rotate your hand so the reel handle is uppermost and your palm faces downward.

With your practice-casting weight hanging about 6 inches (15 cm) below the rod tip, press down on the reel's push button with your right thumb and hold the button down. Bring the rod back over your shoulder so it extends behind you at about a 45-degree angle, then stop for a moment. Check to make

These modern spin-casting reels are set up for right-handed winding.

sure that when you sweep the rod forward in a vertical plane to cast that you're not going to hit anyone or anything nearby. Make sure, too, that you're facing a target. (My children use a bucket on our front lawn as a practice target, with a casting distance of 30 or 40 feet [9 or 12 m].)

Now, sweep the rod forward with a smoothly accelerating stroke and stop abruptly when the rod is about 45-degrees in front of you. At the same instant you stop, let go of the button with your thumb. This releases the line inside the reel so that the practice weight will fly to the target.

It's easy to tell what you're doing wrong if your practice casting doesn't seem to be quite right. If the weight goes in a high arc toward the target as you complete your cast, you're

This father and his son are panfishing in Rutland State Park in Massachusetts.

releasing the button too soon. If the weight shoots down to the ground in front of you, you're releasing the button too late. Ideally the practice weight should go to the target with a low flat trajectory when you release the button at the right moment during the casting stroke. Make sure, by the way, that you practice-cast in a vertical plane. This is more accurate and safer than the sidearm motion that some beginners tend to adopt.

The simple operation of spin-casting reels makes them ideal first reels for small chil-dren, who by age four are usually able to master the casting operation fairly quickly. My fishing friend and neighbor Charlie Olmstead made a game out of casting for his two small children that ended up costing him a small for-tune. To get his kids more interested in practice casting, Charlie set up a plastic bucket as a casting target and put a bunch of quarters in the bucket as an incentive. Every time his son or daughter managed to put the practice plug into the bucket from the pre-scribed casting distance, he or she was given a quarter. The last time I saw him, Charlie told me that nine-year-old Charlotte had quickly earned $27.00, and he was on his way to buy a smaller bucket.

When reeling in line—or retrieving a lure or bait—many people simply hold the rod handle in their left hand without putting any tension on the line and crank the reel handle with their right. This method can create tangles of slack line inside the reel, which, in turn, can require taking the reel apart to untangle the line—a real nuisance. To avoid this common problem, grip the rod just in front of the reel with your left hand after you cast. Your thumb and index finger should be on top of the rod holding the line just in front of the reel; your other three fingers should be under the rod helping to support it and the reel. When you crank in line with your right hand, use the thumb and index finger of your left hand to put a little tension on the incoming line so it will spool evenly onto the reel. This grip also has the additional advantage of allowing your left hand to feel any subtle tap or tug on the line, which is especially important in bait fishing or when fishing with plastic worms for bass.

Most spin-casting reels offer a variable drag based on a slipping-clutch principle. The variable drag allows you to change the tension under which line can be pulled from the spool by a fish. Large trout, bass, walleye, and other fish must be played with drag on the reel, or the line or a knot will break, and you'll lose the fish. As a general rule, set the drag tension to about 20 percent of the line's breaking strength (see page 109) if you're going to be fishing in open water with relatively few obstructions where a heavy fish might tangle or break your line. Professional anglers often set their drags precisely with a spring-loaded scale; you should be able to adjust yours by rough estimate. For large fish in heavy cover, you may want a heavier drag setting, but never exceed a setting of about one-third of the line's rated breaking strength.

Remember that the object of your reel's drag is not to try to stop a big fish in its tracks—which will result in a broken line or knot—but to allow the fish to take line in a controlled fashion and thereby tire itself. Drag adjustment mechanisms vary slightly among reel models; there's usually a small knob on the reel housing or a wheel next to the handle with a printed indication such as a plus and a minus sign to indicate how turning the mechanism adjusts the drag.

Spin-casting reels have been improved dramatically in recent years, particularly with regard to drag-system smoothness and gearing. There are lightweight models, perfect for small trout and panfish, and heavier versions with beefed-up drags and gears for largemouth bass fishing in heavy weeds. Since most spin-casting reels come with line already installed, this can be taken as some indication of how a particular model should be used. Reels spooled with 4- or 6-pound- (1.8- or 2.7-kg-) test monofilament are usually appropriate for small trout, panfish, and even smallmouth bass and walleye in open water. Heavier models are usually spooled with 10-pound-

Spin-casting reels are easy to use, and heavy-duty models are perfect for novices after largemouth bass.

(4.5-kg-) test or heavier line; these are commonly used for largemouth bass and pike in weedy areas where heavier line and a stronger drag are needed to force larger fish away from obstructions in the water.

Although ideal for beginners, spin-casting reels do have their drawbacks. Their basic design limits line capacity, so these reels are generally unsuitable for long-running freshwater fish such as steelhead and salmon. The conical spool cover restricts the flow of line and reduces casting distance slightly compared to other types of reels; this same cover makes it difficult to control the flight of the lure during the cast, which makes these reels somewhat less accurate in casting than other types. And finally, although spin-casting reels are less tangle-prone than other types, when line does become tangled inside them, the cover has to be removed to untangle it. Other types of freshwater reels solve these particular difficulties in different ways, as you'll see in the following chapters.

It is not easy to tell one how to cast. The art must be acquired by practice.

— Charles F. Orvis (1883)

Chapter 2
Spinning Reels

When Alfred Illingworth received a British patent for the first spinning reel in 1905, he couldn't have known that he'd just developed what is now the world's most widely used freshwater reel. For the next forty years or so after Illingsworth's invention, his design wasn't popular at all—the braided linen or silk lines of the era simply didn't work well with his fixed-spool design. The introduction of nylon monofilament line after World War II was a perfect match for the spinning reel, however, and by the mid-1950s there were more than a hundred different spinning-reel brands avail-

able to anglers. The popularity of sport fishing grew enormously in the post-war years, due primarily to the availability of spinning tackle. During this time millions of people discovered this angling method's remarkable versatility and simplicity.

The term spinning, as it applies to a fishing reel, probably borrows its name from the late nineteenth-century textile industry, in which various contrivances were developed to handle large spools of thread, and upon which techniques this reel's design is largely based. In casting and retrieving line, the spinning reel's spool is fixed like spin-casting reels, but is unlike conventional bait-casting and fly reels in which the spool itself is turned to recover line.

In a spinning reel, a line roller attached to a gear-driven cup revolves around a stationary spool. This action winds line on the spool when the reel handle is turned. At the same time, another gear makes the spool oscillate up and down within the cup so the line is

BLUEGILL SUNFISH

Sunfish belong to the same taxonomic family as the freshwater bass, which they superficially resemble. The common bluegill sunfish is perhaps the most widespread of North America's panfishes, and is usually common in the shallow margins of most warm-water ponds and lakes. In spring, they excavate small, bowl-shaped nests that are easily spotted in shoreline shallows. The male bluegill guards the nest aggressively and will nip the toes of a wader who ventures too near. The world-record bluegill exceeds 4 pounds (1.8 kg), but such giants are unusual. The most commonly caught bluegills are 4 to 8 inches (10 to 20 cm) long; anything over 9 inches (22.5 cm) is unusual.

These fish are exceptionally powerful for their small size and are terrific fun to catch on light tackle. They can be taken readily on most small trout flies, but the most sport may be gained with miniature, floating bass bugs made on a size 8 or 10 hook. Ultralight spinning tackle also works well using miniature spinners and spoons in the $\frac{1}{32}$- to $\frac{1}{16}$-ounce (.9- to 1.75-g) range. Small jigs may account for the largest fish, which tend to frequent deeper water, especially during the daylight hours.

wound evenly up and down the spool's depth. This ensures that each succeeding layer of line isn't crammed into the underlying layers, thus allowing line to flow freely over the end of the spool when a lure or bait is cast. Because the line can flow or spin freely over the end of the fixed spool when casting a weight, there is relatively little friction.

The spinning reel (left) mounts under the rod; the bait-casting reel (center) mounts on top.

For this reason, spinning reels make it possible to cast light lures a considerable distance. Ultralight spinning reels, for example, can be used to cast lures weighing as little as

Courtesy Eppinger Mfg. Company

$1/32$ ounce (.9 g)—assuming a correspondingly light (such as 2-pound- [.9-kg-] test) line is used. Casting such light lures is almost impossible with any other type of tackle except for fly tackle. Although light lures and light lines were part of the spinning reels' original appeal, the reels quickly underwent a variety of design modifications to accommodate different kinds of fishing tactics. Now there are spinning-reel models available for catching almost every type of fish—from tiny sunfish to giant sturgeon.

All spinning reels share a number of common features. First, there's a short, solid shaft perpendicular to the reel body that leads to a flat narrow plate parallel to the reel body. This shaft is called the reel "foot." The flat narrow portion of the foot is what fits into the reelseat on the rod. Second, the reel handle is usually on the left side of the reel body for right-handed casters, who normally turn the

A backpacker's fishing tackle often includes easily carried ultralight spinning gear and a small assortment of spoons.

reel handle with their left hand. Left-handers can switch the handle on most reels, which usually allow this same handle to be easily installed on the opposite side of the reel body. Third, many spinning reels have a spool surrounded by a rotating armature that turns around both the spool and a bowl-like extension on the bottom of the spool called a "skirt," as opposed to a traditional cup. Such skirted-spool reels are less prone to tangling because it's harder for loose line to get underneath the spool. Skirted spools, however, tend to be smaller in diameter than regular spools with the same specifications and thus have shorter casting distances. Still, for most fishing this particular disadvantage doesn't make much difference; the tangle-free features of skirted-spool reels have made them very popular.

Both regular and skirted spools have a bail and line roller assembly that looks like a bucket handle (hence the name "bail") around the side of the spool. If you lift the bail upward, you'll feel a click as it fastens and holds in a vertical, open position. After you cast, you can turn the reel handle to click the bail shut. When it shuts, it captures the line and slides it under the line roller. You should make sure your line roller is perfectly smooth—not chipped or scratched—and turns freely if it's designed to do so. Inadequate or damaged line rollers are a primary cause of line failure on spinning reels.

Almost all spinning reels are available with easily interchangeable line spools. This means you can keep in your tacklebox spare spools loaded with lighter or heavier line for use with lighter or heavier lures than those you normally use. It's also an advantage to be able to quickly change to a fresh spool if the one you're using becomes irrevocably snarled when the fishing action is fast and furious. So when selecting a spinning reel, buy one or two extra spools at the same time.

Unlike spin-casting reels, spinning reels usually don't come filled with line. Many tackle shops and a few mail-order houses, however, will use a mechanical line-winding device to fill your reel for a nominal fee. This

Spoons such as these are commonly used with either bait-casting or spinning tackle for a wide variety of game fish.

is the most economical and trouble-free approach, since you'll receive the exact amount of line, correctly installed, without waste and twists. Spare spools also can be filled in the same manner.

Sooner or later, though, you're going to have to spool your own spinning reels. There are a few precautions you should observe to avoid line twist and to ensure top performance. First, mount the reel on the rod. Spinning reels are designed to mount under the rod grip so both the reel and the line guides are on the same side. If the reelseat is in a fixed position, you'll have to use it that way. If the reelseat consists of two sliding rings over a cork or synthetic handle, mount the reel in the middle of the handle, and secure each end of the reel foot with one of the sliding rings. You might later wish to move the reel slightly forward of center for better balance in casting. Now thread the line through the first guide, then use an Arbor Knot (page 123) to secure the line to the reel spool. Be sure to open the bail before you attach the line to the spool so you'll be able to wind on the line after the bail is closed.

At this point, the easiest method to wind on line is to put the line spool flat on the

Courtesy Eppinger Mfg. Company

Courtesy Daiwa Corporation

The little button on top of this spinning-reel's spool is the spool-release latch.

Courtesy G-Loomis

The sliding-ring reelseat on the rod at left is good only for light-tackle angling.

floor, then crank in line with the reel. Be sure the line runs through your fingers under a slight tension as it goes on the reel so that it spools evenly. After a few turns, stop cranking and allow a little slack to fall between the reel and line spool. If the slack line twists, you're taking line off the spool in the wrong direction; you'll need to turn the line spool over to make line come off of it in the opposite direction before you continue cranking.

Be very careful when filling the reel spool to avoid both slack winds on the reel spool

and twisting the line. If either happens, your reel will be plagued by frequent and annoying line tangles.

Continue filling the reel spool until it's filled to within ⅛ inch (3 mm) of the rim. Spools filled more than this tend to release loops of slack line when you cast, and thus cause tangles. Spools filled with too little line will reduce your effective casting distance due to the friction caused by line rubbing against the spool rim.

When your reel spool is full, cut the line

© Kenneth Martin/Amstock

Walleyes such as this are popular targets for spin fishermen.

and secure the loose end on the spool with a rubber band until you are ready to go fishing. Now you can fill your spare spools with the same or different size line. After each spool is full, mark a small piece of tape with the line weight and its installation date, then fasten it to the underside of the spool in such a way that the tape won't interfere with the spool's operation. The information on the tape is essential when you check or change your line and—if you have more than one spool for the same reel—also enables you to keep track of what types of line are on your spare spools.

All spinning reels have an anti-reverse feature. This keeps the handle from turning backward and whacking your knuckles when you hook a strong fish, and ensures that the fish pulls against the reel's drag. This same feature also helps to keep the bail from closing unexpectedly when you're casting; if this happens when you're using a heavy lure, the line may snap and you'll lose the lure. The anti-reverse feature on most reels is turned on and off with a sliding switch or lever at the

The initial, smashing strike and leap of a largemouth bass is one of the great moments in angling.

© Wally Eberhart

rear of the reel body. You should leave your anti-reverse on at all times unless you have a specific reason for not doing so.

Drag is adjusted on most spinning reels by means of a knob on top of the reel spool. On some reels, this adjustment is at the rear-most portion of the reel body. In either case, turning the knob clockwise tightens the drag, while a counterclockwise turn loosens the drag. As with most other reel types, set your drag to 25 or 30 percent of your line's rated breaking strength. This will allow a strong fish to pull line from the reel in a controlled fashion without breaking it.

Never try to increase the drag adjustment while you're playing a fish. Instead apply additional drag tension by using the fingers of your left hand as a brake against the reel spool; if the fish makes a sudden lunge, you can release the extra tension instantly and avoid a broken line.

Casting with a spinning reel is almost as easy as with a spin-casting reel and can be much more accurate. String the line through the guides and use a Trilene Knot (page 123) to attach a snap swivel (page 121) to the end of the line. Then attach a practice-casting weight that is an appropriate size for your outfit. A ¼-ounce (7-g) weight is good for most medium-weight rods and reels.

Now, hold the rod and reel in your right hand with the reel stem between your second and third fingers. Reel the practice weight up to within 4 or 6 inches (10 or 15 cm) of the rod tip. Use your right index finger to hold the line while your left hand cocks the bail open. Make sure the line is resting on the fleshy part of your fingertip and isn't caught down in the finger's first joint. (Some spinning reels have a trigger device on the bail

© Wally Eberhart

Spin-fishing for trout often means light lines and ultra-small lures.

hit anything when you bring the rod forward. Now aim at a target 30 or 40 feet (9 or 12 m) in the distance, and bring the rod sharply and smoothly forward. When the rod is at about a 45-degree angle in front of you, stop abruptly and simultaneously release the line. The practice weight will fly through the air as soon as you release the line held by your right index finger.

Once again, it is easy to tell what's going wrong when you are having casting problems. If the weight goes out in a high looping trajectory on the cast, you're letting go of the line too soon. If the weight darts into the ground in front of you, you're releasing too late. As with most lure-type casts, the practice weight should go to the target in a low flat trajectory.

Spinning reels do offer the advantage of being able to control the flight of the lure to a certain extent. If it appears that you're going to overshoot the target, just extend your right index finger to the lip of the spool to slow the line as it comes off of it, which will shorten the cast in midair. Many experts can hit a coffee cup consistently at 60 feet (18 m) with spinning gear—such accuracy can be very important in many kinds of fishing. Your own practice can pay big dividends.

One common mistake anglers make when fishing with spinning reels is turning the reel handle while a large fish is pulling line against the drag system. Doing so will usually twist the line so badly that you'll have to throw the line away. Remember, retrieve line only when the fish is coming toward you.

that allows you to capture the line with your right index finger and open the bail simultaneously with the same finger.)

Now, bring the rod gently back overhead until it points at a 45-degree angle behind you. Look around to make sure you won't

Being out in the woods fishing is one of the few places left on earth where a man can find solitude without loneliness.

—John Voelker (writing as Robert Traver)

Chapter 3
Bait-casting Reels

Modern bait-casting reels are engineering marvels, but perhaps no more so than the first such reel, made by George Snyder, a Kentucky watchmaker, in 1810. Snyder's reel differed from earlier brass British reels in two important respects. First, his reel was sufficiently smooth-running, which meant that a bait could be cast from the reel itself. Earlier reels were so rough that line had to be pulled from the reel, held, and then released by hand in order to cast. Second, Snyder's reel was also a multiplier; that is, the line spool revolved more than once for every turn of the reel handle, unlike earlier reels, all of which were single-action (the spool revolved once for every turn of the handle). Bait-casting reels soon came to be 4:1 multipliers, with four spool revolutions per handle turn; some modern models offer even higher ratios. Soon there were other watchmakers in the reel trade, notably C. F. Millam, J. F. Meek, and B. F. Meek, and by the end of the American Civil War these reels had become an angling standard.

These early reels were first used for fishing with bait, hence the name bait-casting. When bass plugs came into vogue after 1900, the same reels were often called plug-casting reels. Today bait-casting reels are used for many types of fishing, and are often referred to as casting or conventional reels.

Bait-casting reels are more difficult to operate and therefore require more skill to use than spin-casting or spinning reels. However, many anglers find mastering this skill to be especially rewarding because these reels offer the greatest casting accuracy, allow use of

Courtesy Daiwa Corporation

Modern bait-casting reels are often sleek, well-engineered marvels for the ultimate in casting accuracy.

Courtesy Daiwa Corporation

Different bait-casting reel sizes should be matched to the fish you expect to catch.

© Kenneth Martin/Amstock

heavier line for a given lure weight, and are the most efficient fighting tools when coping with large fish. Because the spool revolves when the lure or bait is pulling out line during the cast, the spool itself can overrun, and, if not controlled, will produce a line tangle called a backlash. You avoid backlashes by employing precise thumb control of the spool when casting. Most modern reels have built-in mechanical anti-backlash devices that help somewhat in this regard, but no such device completely eliminates the need for a practiced thumb when casting.

Like spin-casting reels, bait-casting reels are mounted on top of a rod with a trigger-type reelseat. These reels have a flat elongated foot that fits into the reelseat. A screw-locking device or clamp holds the foot securely to

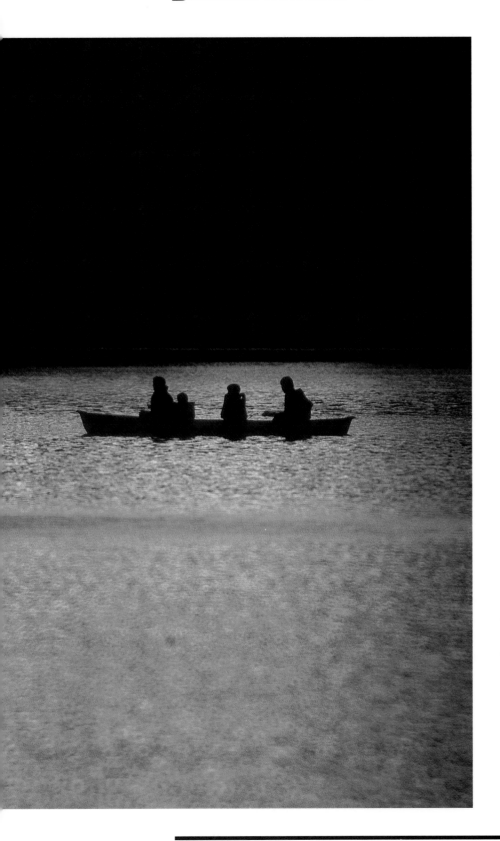

the reelseat. A right-handed reel has its handle on the right side when correctly mounted. Almost all bait-casting reels feature a level-wind device that moves back and forth in front of the spool when the reel handle is turned, ensuring that the line is evenly spooled on the reel. You may eventually encounter a bait-casting reel without such a device, but be forewarned that these are for experts only.

Changing spools on bait-casting reels involves unscrewing and removing one side-plate, and is a general pain in the neck on most models. Over the years, I've found it simpler to have a complete spare reel on hand, instead of trying to change spools.

Bait-casting reels don't come filled with line and, again, the easiest thing is to have the reel filled at the store or by the mail-order firm where you buy the reel. Of course, you're going to have to do this yourself eventually, so here's how. You'll need to find someone to assist you.

First, mount the reel on the rod. Thread the line through the rod guides, then through the level-wind device, and fasten it to the reel spool with an Arbor Knot (page 123). Have your helper poke a pencil or similar object through the small hole in the center of the line spool so the spool can revolve on this axis when you're cranking the reel handle. Your helper should apply a slight and constant tension to the line spool while you're winding so the line spools on the reel evenly.

When filling the spool, make sure the line spool and reel spool are both turning in the same direction to avoid line twist. If they're not, turn the line spool around and then continue. Keep cranking until the spool is filled to within $\frac{1}{8}$ to $\frac{1}{16}$ inch (3 to 1.6 mm) of the spool's edge, then clip the line and secure the loose end with a rubber band until you are ready to use your rod and reel.

Like other reels, filling a bait-casting reel with too little line reduces casting efficiency, and using too much line produces tangles. Overfilling bait-casting reels may also allow slack line to slip between the reel spool and the frame—and you'll have to take the reel apart to solve this problem if and when it occurs. Premium reels minimize this problem since they are made exactly to fine specifications and have very little space between their reel spools and frames.

Today, most bait-casting reels have a free-spool button or similar device at the right rear of the reel frame. This mechanism disengages the handle and drive gears when a cast is made; it also allows the spool to turn more freely, thus producing smoother and longer casts. There should also be—and usually is—a built-in anti-reverse mechanism that keeps the handle from turning backward and rapping your knuckles when reeling in or fighting a fish. If your anti-reverse can be turned on and off, leave it on all the time.

Almost all bait-casting reels have a star drag that is adjusted with a star-shaped wheel be-tween the reel handle and sideplate, and should be set to 25 to 30 percent of your line's rated breaking strength. As usual, don't try to change the drag adjustment when you're fighting a fish. It's very simple to apply additional pressure on the reel spool with your thumb to put more pressure on a fish. Since you can release your thumb almost instantly, you won't risk losing the fish when it suddenly heads for the next county. This type of supplemental drag and precise control is most easily done with bait-casting reels and is a big advantage when fishing for big largemouth bass, northern pike, muskies, and even salmon or steelhead. If I were fishing for a trophy fish of any kind and wanted to be most certain of landing it, I'd use a bait-casting reel.

Casting with a bait-casting reel is more complicated than with a spinning or spin-casting reel, but the reward is well worth the time and effort. To prepare to practice-cast, start by threading the line through the rod guides and using a Trilene Knot (page 123) to attach a snap swivel (page 121) to the end of the line. For most medium-weight outfits, beginners will find a $\frac{3}{8}$-ounce (10.5-g) practice weight easier than the $\frac{1}{4}$-ounce (7-g) weight suggested for spinning or spin-casting. If you have a heavier rig for northern pike or muskies, use a heavier weight—$\frac{5}{8}$ ounce (17.5 g), or even more in proportion to your outfit.

Now, reel the weight up to within 6 inches (15 cm) of the rod tip. Adjust your cast-control knob (anti-backlash device) so that when the

Bait-casting reels are American classics, dating back to reels made by Kentucky watchmakers in the early 1800s.

reel is in the free-spool position the weight will descend *slowly* to the ground. If the casting weight won't descend of its own accord, your setting is too light. If it moves rapidly downward, your setting is too heavy; tighten your cast control slightly and try again. If you're practicing on a windy day, set yourself up to cast with the wind at your back. Your target should be 40 feet (12 m) away.

Grip the rod in your right hand with the reel handle on top, your right index finger on the reelseat trigger, and your right thumb resting on the lowermost edge of the reel spool. Press your thumb against the spool to keep it from moving while you press the free-spool button with your left hand. Then raise your forearm and bend your wrist to bring the rod behind you to a 45-degree angle.

Now, bring the rod sharply forward with a chopping motion of your arm and wrist, then stop abruptly when the rod is 45 degrees in front of you. As you stop, release *almost* all of your thumb pressure against the spool. If you remove your thumb completely from the spool it will overrun and backlash. If you press too hard against the spool, it won't turn and the casting weight won't go anywhere. The lightest pressure of your thumb will help you keep control of the turning spool. This "touch" comes with practice. (Even superb anglers and champion tournament casters get their share of backlashes.) The development of the proper touch is the most important—and difficult—aspect of bait-casting to master. As

Bait-casting reels (top) are mounted above the rod while spinning reels (bottom) are mounted below, which is one of several basic differences between the two types.

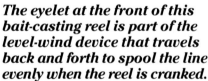

The eyelet at the front of this bait-casting reel is part of the level-wind device that travels back and forth to spool the line evenly when the reel is cranked.

the casting weight flies to the target, its speed diminishes. The speed of the rotating reel spool, however, diminishes more slowly than the weight itself. If you don't thumb the spool and control its rotation during the cast, you'll backlash. Gradually increase your thumb pressure during the cast so the spool stops at the same instant the weight does.

The beauty of this method is that you're in complete control of the cast at all times. You can stop the casting weight (or lure or bait) at any point in its flight with simple thumb pressure and thus be exceptionally accurate. With practice, you will become acquainted with the feel of your reel and greatly improve your casting.

Backlashes can rival a bird's nest in com-

plexity, and it takes plenty of patience and practice to untangle them. Of course, the time and place to practice is a quiet afternoon on the lawn, not in a boat watching bass chase minnows all over the cove. Some beginners may find it helpful to tighten the cast control on their reels more than normal when starting out, then loosen that control to a lighter, more appropriate setting as they gain proficiency. The greatest difficulty comes in casting light lures or baits. These require the most finely attuned thumb. Casting into a stiff breeze is also troublesome, since the wind will slow the lure's flight prematurely and your reel-thumbing will have to compensate for this. If you are fishing in a strong head wind, you will probably want to switch to spinning tackle.

After you cast, switch the reel and rod to your left hand. Cup the left side of the reel against your palm and use your left thumb and index finger to apply a little tension to the line as you retrieve your casting weight.

© Arthur Tilley/FPG International

Largemouth bass are probably the most popular quarry sought with bait-casting reels, which are also suitable for smallmouths, pike, muskies, walleye, and other game fish.

Support the rod with the remaining three fingers of your left hand under the reel and rod while you turn the reel handle with your right hand. (This grip is called a palming grip because of the position of your left hand.) Alternatively, and with bait-casting rods that have a fairly long (or two-handed) rear grip, you can use your left hand to hold the rod on the small grip forward of the reel, while you use your thumb and forefinger on that hand to apply tension as just described. In this case the butt of the rod should be braced against your lower abdomen.

Bait-casting reels are used most effectively with heavier line weights and lures. The lighter the line and lure, the harder it is to cast with these reels. The reels readily adapt to heavier lines (10- to 25-pound- [4.5- to 11.3-kg-] test) by virtue of their revolving spools. While heavy lines diminish the effectiveness of fixed-spool spinning reels through friction, the friction factor of a revolving spool is the same regardless of line size within reasonable limits, and the angler's options are correspondingly greater.

Bait-casting reels now come in a wide variety of sizes, from ultralight models, which weigh in at around 8 ounces (224 g), to large casting and freshwater trolling reels that may weigh 20 ounces (560 g) and more. In general, a model suitable for freshwater bass, pike, and walleye fishing will weigh close to 9 ounces (252 g), accommodate about 200 yards (180 m) of 10-pound- (4.5-kg-) test monofilament, and have a gear ratio of 4:1 or 5:1.

WALLEYE

Walleye are the largest member of the perch family, and are found in many larger lakes and rivers throughout the United States and Canada. They are also one of the tastiest fish that swim, which accounts in large measure for their broad popularity. They are common in some areas of the Great Lakes, particularly Lake Erie. The "walleye" name refers to a special area of the fish's retina that is especially sensitive to light and is reflective, much like the eye of a cat. For this reason, in clear water they are usually found deep during daylight hours.

Walleye have been recorded at 25 pounds (11.25 kg), but only reach such sizes in southern reservoirs that offer abundant food and a long growing season. Most walleye that are caught weigh from 1 to 3 pounds (.45 to 1.35 kg) and 14 to 24 inches (35 to 60 cm) long. Sometimes called walleyed pike, these fish are, in fact, no relation to true pike.

Walleye are usually found in schools, which can mean fast action for a time after they're located. They generally feed on smaller fish, although both angleworms and leeches are also used as natural baits. Medium-weight spinning outfits are most commonly used to cast or troll assorted minnow-type swimming plugs. By early summer in many waters, walleye are feeding heavily on young-of-the-year yellow perch, which can make perch-color plugs effective. Plastic grubs on leadhead jigs, sometimes tipped with a minnow, are effective in deeper waters.

Reels have been greatly improved in shape of late years; they are now made much deeper, and not so broad, thus allowing the line to be run off more easily, and be wound up more quickly.

— William Stewart (1857)

Chapter 4
Fly Reels

With the various types of freshwater tackle discussed in previous chapters, a weighted lure is used in casting to pull line from the reel. Fly-casting works in just the opposite way. In this case, a nearly weightless fly or bug is carried through the air by a heavy line; in other words, the line itself is the casting weight and the fly goes along for the ride. Among other things, this means that fly reels aren't used for casting at all and, for most freshwater applications, are the simplest of all reels.

Fly reels have three essential functions in fly fishing. They provide adequate storage space for a bulky fly line that is pulled from the reel by hand before the cast is made. They allow larger fish to be played from the reel and may even incorporate a drag system for this purpose. They serve to counterbalance the weight of the fly rod that extends for many feet beyond the angler's hand and reel.

Fly reels are generally narrow in proportion to their diameter, and most are "ventilated" with numerous holes drilled in the sideplates. Such ventilation was originally done to aid the air-drying of older silk fly lines that rotted if they weren't dried after use. With modern synthetic lines, these holes serve no real purpose except to generally lighten the reel. The reel spool revolves on a central spindle, which should be kept clean and lightly lubricated for optimal performance. Fly-reel spools are easily interchangeable; since many fly-casters use more than one line type (floating and sinking versions, for example), a spare spool is desirable.

Make sure that the small latch that holds the fly-reel spool in the reel frame is secure

These single-action fly reels are typically narrow in proportion to their diameter, which allows the line to be retrieved relatively quickly.

Courtesy Orvis Company, Inc.

every time you use the reel. Perry Chibbs, an old friend who lives near Toronto and often fly-fishes for large pike in northern Ontario, recently sent me a photograph that showed not only a huge pike, but also his heavily bandaged hand. As he explained in his letter: "I finally hooked this pike on a big streamer fly—a fish I'd been trying for all summer—and the fish ran hard for the other side of Haskill's Cove. Suddenly, the fly-reel spool popped loose and started spinning and clanking like mad on the boat floor. I tried grabbing the loose spool while the fish was pulling line, and the spool edges sliced up my hand. I finally had to just play the fish gently with the line in my hands. It was just dumb luck landing it after the reel came apart."

Most fly reels are of a single-action design, which means that the reel spool revolves once for every turn of the handle. A few fly-reel models have multiplying gears, or multipliers, that allow line to be reeled in more quickly. Since the line isn't being reeled up after every cast, however, multipliers are almost superfluous (although salmon and steelhead anglers sometimes find them useful).

There are also some automatic fly reels that work on a principle similar to a window shade: The action of pulling line out for casting winds a spring inside the reel. A lever can then be actuated to rewind the line on the reel rapidly. Automatic reels are helpful when bass bugging from a canoe or boat because they allow easy control of large amounts of slack line. Their relatively high weight and small line capacity, however, makes them of little use when fishing along a trout stream or salmon river.

Fly reels are designed to be mounted under the rod and at the rear with the reelseat behind the rod grip. The winding handle may be on the right or left side as you prefer. Try using the reel with its handle on the left side first so you don't have to switch the rod from your right to your left hand to wind up line or play a fish. On most rods, the reel foot locks into the reelseat by means of threaded rings; some lighter models have a pair of sliding bands for the same purpose. There are a few fly reels whose feet don't fit all reelseats. This is less common now than in past years, but it still pays to make sure that your new reel will fit on your new rod before you buy either.

Courtesy Orvis Company, Inc.

Like many other reel types, fly reels come in a wide range of sizes. Remember that small trout reels don't have sufficient line capacity for salmon fishing, for example.

To fill your fly reel with line, you'll probably have to use some backing, as most fly lines are only about 90 feet (27 m) long. Backing is a fine-diameter line spooled on the reel under the fly line that will allow you to handle large, long-running fish, and also ensures that the reel itself is filled to capacity. If the reel is only partly full, the effective circumference of the spool will be reduced and you'll retrieve line at a slower rate. A partly filled spool also means the fly line will be stored in smaller coils, which the line tends to retain after being pulled from the spool for casting.

Most reel makers specify how much backing a particular reel will accommodate in addition to a fly line of a certain size. This makes it relatively easy to fill a reel. If you don't know how much backing your reel will take, the most accurate way of filling the reel is to first wind on the fly line, then wind backing on top of the fly line until the reel is full. Then you'll have to reverse the lines so the backing is underneath the fly line. Let's assume for the moment that the information supplied with your reel has stated its capacity.

It's easiest to fill your reel when it's on the rod. First, mount your reel; thread the backing line through the first butt guide, and attach it to the reel spool with an Arbor Knot (page 123). Use 20-pound- (9-kg-) test braided Dacron™ backing line sold specifically for this purpose. Ask a friend to poke a pencil or sim-

The open-frame, or palming-rim, design of this reel allows you to add drag by pressing your fingertips against the edge of the spool when a fish is pulling the line.

ilar object through the backing-line spool and apply a little tension to the line while you wind it on the reel. If you're winding with your left hand, use the fingers of your right to move the line back and forth as you wind so the line spools on the reel evenly. Make sure the backing spool and reel spool are turning in the same direction to avoid line twist.

When the right amount of backing is spooled (again, see the instructions that came with your reel), clip the line and attach the fly line to the backing with an Albright Knot (page 123). Most new fly lines have a small tag on one end that indicates which end should be attached to the backing. (With some lines, if you attach the wrong end, the fly-line taper will be reversed and you won't be able to cast it very well.) Now wind on the fly line as you did the backing (with a pencil through the line spool), being careful to avoid line twist. The entire fly line should fit on the reel to within ⅛ inch (3 mm) or so of the spool edge. The spool should turn freely without any line binding against the reel frame.

If the entire line doesn't fit, don't cut it. Its continuous taper is important in your casting. Instead, remove the fly line, then remove enough backing so you can install the complete fly line.

Next, you should attach a leader to the fly line. A leader is a tapered length of monofilament from 7½ to 12 feet (2.25 to 3.6 m) long that provides the nearly invisible link between fly line and fly. Its taper helps the fly to "turn

over," that is, lie straight out from the line at the end of a cast. The butt end (thickest portion) of the leader should be attached to the end of the fly line with a Nail Knot (page 123).

Most fly reels have a simple, click-type drag system based on a triangular metal pawl that is held against a gear on the back of the spool by a light spring. This type of drag makes the reel click in both directions and offers slightly more resistance to outgoing line than when the line is reeled in. On many reels this click tension is adjustable, and should be set only tight enough to prevent the reel from overrunning when you give a sudden jerk on the line. Your fingers can provide additional tension when you're playing a fish. You can either

Courtesy Orvis Company, Inc.

This fly reel is shown correctly mounted (for right-handed winding) on the fly-rod reelseat behind the rod grip.

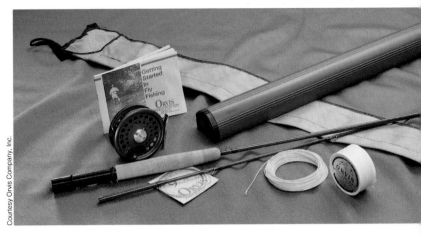

Courtesy Orvis Company, Inc.

Most major fly-tackle makers offer complete outfits, including rod, reel, fly line, and backing line, that are often less expensive than individually purchased components.

clamp the line down against the rod grip, or use your fingers to put pressure against the inside of the spool. In either case, you'll find the sensitivity of your hand and fingers offers a responsive drag.

Some reels have more sophisticated drag systems that are based on the compression of internal drag washers, or have caliper-based systems that work much like the disc brakes on a car. With these types of systems, the drag adjustment should be light; that is, it should be only tight enough to keep the spool from overrunning. Many fly anglers make the mistake of using much too tight a drag setting. This makes little difference for little fish, but when a really big one is hooked the high drag setting will almost certainly cause the hook to pull free or a knot to fail. Again, the best way of applying additional drag is with your fingertips on the line or spool.

It's important that the size of your reel be matched to the rest of your fly tackle. A big steelhead or salmon reel is obviously out of place on a little trout rod—the huge weight near your hand would feel awkward with a small rod—and vice versa. A typical trout-fly reel is 3 to 3.5 inches (7.5 to 8.75 cm) in diameter, and weighs about 4 ounces (112 g) before the addition of line and backing. This type of reel would match well with trout rods that are 7 to 9 feet (2.1 to 2.7 m) long and use WF5F to WF6F lines. (See Chapter 13 for fly-line descriptions.)

PART II
RODS

Like a good fishing reel, a modern rod can be a lifetime investment. With reasonable and minimal care, plus some caution in use, there's no reason why any first-quality fishing rod shouldn't provide decades of service. Rods of inferior quality are a poor choice, whether you're a beginner trying to save money, or a friend buying a gift for a novice to see if he or she likes the sport. Such rods inevitably perform poorly and are a handicap in learning how to fish.

Most modern rods are made of graphite fiber, or graphite fiber combined with fiberglass filaments. In both types of rods, long filaments are combined with epoxy and other thermosetting resins to form a long, hollow tube, called the rod blank. The manufacturer then adds guides, ferrules (joints), and a reelseat that correspond to the type of rod—spinning, spin-casting/bait-casting, or fly. The taper and relative flexibility of the rod blank largely determine the rod's action, that is, the way in which the rod bends when cast with a certain weight lure, bait, or, in the case of fly rods, line.

Fishing rods almost never break in normal use. The most common way rods break is by being shut in a car door. The second most common is in a household door, one that springs shut on the rod while it's being carried outside. And throwing your unprotected rod in the car trunk until the next time you fish almost guarantees that there won't be a next time—at least for that particular rod. Many premium rods come with a rigid, protective tube. If you have one, that's where the rod should live when you're not fishing. You can also make your own inexpensive case from large-diameter plastic plumbing pipe sold at the local hardware store.

Certainly, choosing the right rod from the hundreds displayed in a modern tackle store can be a bewildering experience. The chapters in this section are designed to help you evaluate the basic choices. If you're an enthusiastic angler you may soon wind up like best-selling author and fisherman Robert Traver, who once said that any angler who knew how many rods he had didn't have enough of them.

Fishing is one of the few pursuits left to man that is fun even to fail at.

— John Voelker (writing as Robert Traver)

Chapter 5
Spinning Rods

Modern spinning rods for freshwater fishing may range in length from 4 to 7 feet (1.2 to 2.1 m) or more. In general, the shorter a rod is, the lighter the lure it's designed to cast—although this isn't a hard and fast rule. It is important to remember that every rod is designed to perform best with a lure of a specific weight, so that if you use lighter or heavier lures, your casting performance will be diminished.

Most manufacturers put a label on the rod butt near the grip that specifies an appropriate lure-weight range and often indicates a line-size range as well. You can also find this information at your local tackle shop, and in most mail-order catalogs. For example, a 6½-foot (1.95-m), two-piece spinning rod classified by the maker as light indicates that the rod should be used with 2- to 6-pound- (.9- to 2.7-kg-) test line for lures weighing ⅛ to ½ ounce (3.5 to 14 g). Unfortunately, these specifications can be very misleading, so you'll have to be very careful when selecting a rod on the basis of such labels. It is impossible to build a spinning rod that will cast ⅛- and ½-ounce (3.5- and 14-g) lures equally well (in spite of this particular maker's claim); and while 2- to 6-pound- (.9- to 2.7-kg-) test line might be fine for ⅛-ounce (3.5-g) lures, such lines are impractical for ½-ounce (14-g) baits.

The best possible solution is to take your own spinning reel filled with your preferred line and a practice weight to your tackle shop, and talk the proprietor into letting you test-cast several rods. You'll immediately find which rods are best suited to the rest of your

© Wally Eberhart

tackle, your own casting style, and your particular method of fishing. (If I find a rod I especially like by this method, I usually buy two of them in case one is eventually broken or the manufacturer discontinues that model.)

Many people–mail-order customers, for example–won't be able to do this, however, and the next best approach is an educated reading of the rod's label. If a range of lure weights is specified, the narrowest range is likely to be the most accurate. In the previous example, there's a 400 percent difference between the ⅛- and ½-ounce (3.5- and 14-g) lures specified, which is too much. A range of ⅛ to ¼ ounce (3.5 to 7 g) is more realistic, as is any range with a span of no more than ¼ ounce (7 g).

If the range specified on the rod or in the catalog is a wide one–say ¼ to ⅝ ounce (7 to 17.5 g)–it's generally a fair bet that the mid-

The electric motor on this boat's bow allows a quiet approach to spook fish in shallow water.

dle of that range will bring optimum performance from that particular rod. Note that this discussion has been based on lure weight and *not* line size, which many rod makers also specify. Lure weight is what bends the rod in casting and, in that respect, is independent of line weight. Using the correct weight line is simple common sense: heavy line goes with heavy rods and lures, and light line goes with light rods and lures.

Spinning rods are uniquely characterized by fairly large diameter line guides that form a rapidly decreasing cone when viewed from butt to rod tip. The design of fixed-spool spinning reels is such that in casting, the line

© Kenneth Martin/Amstock

Trout can often be found along the edges of the swift currents in large rivers.

comes off the reel in large open spirals that slap against the rod blank, which creates friction and diminishes the cast. The large guides on a spinning-rod butt are designed to capture the wide line spirals and quickly reduce them to a straight line motion for maximum casting efficiency. Guides, of course, also distribute the tension along the rod's length so it bends evenly when casting and fighting fish. Of course, the guides must be properly spaced on the rod, but I won't bother to describe this fur-

ther because a commercial spinning rod with badly placed guides is now a rare occurrence.

Today, almost all spinning-rod guides are of premium makes, so guide quality needn't be an object of great concern as long as you're dealing with a major-brand rod. As such, the guides usually will be made of hardened metal or have super-hard ceramic inserts to prevent line wear. You should check periodically to make sure the guide inserts aren't cracked (which can occur from a sharp blow), and that the metal guides are likewise undamaged. (One old trick is to slip a piece of nylon stocking or panty hose through the guides. This sensitive material will help you to feel

BROWN TROUT

First introduced in New York and Michigan from Europe in the 1880s, brown trout are now well established in many trout waters throughout North America. In general, they are the most difficult of all trout to catch. The habit of smaller browns—less than 2 pounds (.9 kg) or so—of feeding on stream insects endears this species to fly anglers in particular. Larger browns tend to feed mostly on forage fish and other large quarry such as crayfish. The world-record brown trout is close to 40 pounds (18 kg), and 20- to 30-pound (9- to 13.5-kg) fish have been taken in North American waters; a 5-pound (2.25-kg) brown trout is a trophy on most waters.

The key factor in catching browns is stealth on the angler's part, as these fish are extremely wary. Even the ripples caused by a wading angler or the shadow thrown by a boat can send them into cover and off the bite. Keep a low profile, wade slowly enough to avoid rippling the water, and avoid sudden movements to ensure success.

Larger brown trout are often nocturnal in many rivers and lakes, making dawn and dusk the best fishing times. Favorite lures are 3- to 6-inch-(7.5- to 15-cm-) long minnow-style swimming plugs with a gold and black finish. Although no single fly pattern will work all of the time for these trout, one of the best flies is a Muddler Minnow, which comes in a wide range of sizes.

A tackle-shop display of spinning rods and reels. Make sure your outfit is balanced for the kind of fishing you're doing, neither too heavy nor too light.

Courtesy Cabela's

any nicks or cracks.) In either case, the guide may start to fray and weaken your line, or it may fail totally, which could cause a concentration of bending stress and break your rod.

Reelseats on spinning rods are either of the fixed (screw-locking) or sliding-band variety. If you have a screw-locking seat, you only have to check periodically while fishing to make sure the locking ring has remained tight. This is especially important after the outfit has been transported in a vehicle with the reel mounted, since the vibrations of a car will tend to loosen the reelseat. It's very disconcerting to have the reel come off the rod while you're casting or playing a fish. And it's even more silly (when it happens) than it sounds, but it *can* happen.

Rods with sliding-band reelseats are usually of the ultralight variety in which the reelseat is subject to the least stress. Use the sliding rings on either side of the reel foot to clamp the reel to the rod grip slightly forward of center. If the reel is to be left on the rod for an extended period, you can use electrician's tape to keep the bands from working loose, as they tend to do with time and use.

Graphite fiber, either as a primary component or in combination with fiberglass, is the basis for most modern spinning rods. Spinning rods are typically tip-action rods. These evolved from the needs of bass anglers who needed a light tip to cast small lures as well as a powerful butt section to facilitate hook setting and playing largemouths in heavy

© Kenneth Martin/Amstock

Spinfishermen casting from shore can often score well by broadcasting a series of casts over a wide area from a point of land that juts out into a lake.

cover. Usually, the greater the percentage of graphite in a rod's composition, the more expensive the rod will be. Fiberglass rods are usually at the low end of the price range but shouldn't be overlooked as they do offer some advantages. Other features being equal, fiberglass flexes more easily than graphite; these "softer" rods are a big plus when casting ultralight lures and baits that are just too light to bend a stiffer graphite model. Also, the quicker casting stroke demanded by stiffer graphite models can snap natural baits such as worms or minnows right off the hook, which happens less often with the more forgiving fiberglass rods.

That fish did things to me. I couldn't get the feel of its resistance from my mind nor could I forget how huge and beautiful it looked, glistening in the sunlight. At that moment was born an enthusiastic bass fisherman....

—Ray Bergman

Chapter 6
Bait-casting and Spin-casting Rods

Bait-casting and spin-casting rods have become synonymous, although this wasn't always the case. Both usually featured an offset reelseat set slightly below the line of the rod grip and rod. However, spin-casting rods also had a slight downward bend to the rear grip, which had the net effect of placing the caster's thumb closer to the spin-casting reel's push-button release. By the early 1970s, handle designs became more standardized. Now most single-handed bait-casting rods have both the offset reelseat and slightly decurbed (bent downward) handle, and can be used interchangeably with spin-casting and bait-casting reels as long as the other components of the outfit are in proportion to each other.

Most single-handed bait-casting and spin-casting rods are 5 to 6 feet (1.5 to 1.8 m) long; two-handed versions are usually 6 to 7 feet (1.8 to 2.1 m) long. Single-handed rods are usually of a one-piece design in which even the handle is permanently mounted on the rod blank. Two-handed rods are often two pieces joined by a ferrule in the middle; they are sometimes designed so that the rod telescopes slightly in and out of the handle, reducing the overall length for transport and storage. Two-handed rods are usually, but not always, of a heavier action and designed for larger lures and stronger lines.

Bait-casting and spin-casting rods are characterized by a distinctive trigger-type reelseat and relatively small line guides. The "trigger"

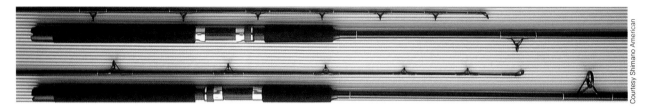

Courtesy Shimano American

Larger bait-casting reels are often used on downrigger (deep-trolling) rods (above).

The bait-casting rod (near right) has a two-handed grip; the other one (far right) has an offset single-handed grip.

Courtesy Daiwa Corporation

is much like the trigger on a gun, held by the index finger of the casting hand, and is a substantial help in supporting the rod during casting. Because spin-casting, and to a greater extent bait-casting, reels must be manipulated with the thumb while casting, both these rods feature offset reelseats that put the reel closer to the thumb, yet still allow a reasonable one-handed grip. Two-handed rods have a longer rear grip for two-handed support in casting heavier lures and usually have straight grips. Note that the bent rear grips on many single-handed bait-casting rods won't fit in rod holders mounted on many boats for trolling. If you're planning to troll as well as cast with your rod, check for fit first.

Guides on bait-casting rods can be relatively small since line comes off a bait-casting reel in a straight line when casting. The same is generally true of spin-casting reels, as the reel's cone reduces the size of the line loops before they reach the guides. As usual, check your guides periodically for cracks or breaks that could wear your line or cause the guide to fail.

Courtesy Daiwa Corporation

Here's the gamut of bait-casting rods. The upper rods are for lighter lures and lines, and the lower rods are for heavy-tackle bass fishing and larger game fish.

Additionally, bait-casting rods also have the stiff actions bass anglers prefer, thanks in part to the increased popularity of both graphite-fiber rods and professional bass tournaments by the 1970s. This means that the lure accelerates very rapidly during the casting stroke and, therefore, a skilled thumb is required on the revolving spool to avoid backlashes. Fiberglass and some fiberglass/graphite composite rods may have softer, deeper-flexing actions, and are much easier to cast with lures of the appropriate weight. If you're buying your first bait-casting rod, ask the tackle sales-person for the softest-action rod for your desired lure weight. This will make learning to cast much easier.

Softer-action rods can also be more accurate. I first learned this from a bass angler with the improbable name of Slider Schultz, a nickname—I later learned—he'd earned for his ability to cast his bass plugs under overhanging branches and other obstructions. We were fishing the shoreline of a bass lake in southern New Jersey, and Slider was catching two or three bass to every one that I hooked. After a while I stopped fishing and just watched.

As the boat moved slowly along, it was obvious that his plug was landing much closer to the shoreline than mine. He was lobbing his plug under branches and next to stumps with incredible accuracy. I tried again and still couldn't do it.

CRAPPIES

Crappies are a widely distributed and popular panfish that grow somewhat larger than bluegills and are delicious eating. They are found in warm-water lakes and ponds all over the United States, although their distribution is most limited in the Rocky Mountain states. There are two common species: black crappies and white crappies. The fish are essentially similar, although the black variety tends to be randomly speckled and the white species' speckling tends toward a vertical barring. Both species may reach weights of 5 or 6 pounds (2.25 or 2.7 kg), but are usually 8 to 12 inches (20 to 30 cm) long and weigh up to a pound (.45 kg). Crappies are well known for a cyclical population, that is, a few years of excellent crappie fishing are typically followed by a few seasons when it's hard to find even one.

Crappies typically associate themselves with lake structure such as brush piles or weedbeds. They feed primarily on smaller fish, including their own young. They are also a schooling fish, which means you're apt to catch a large number of them once you find the right spot. Ultralight spinning lures are often a favorite choice; spoons, spinners, and small plastic grubs all work well at times. A slow and erratic retrieve may be necessary to tease crappies into striking, but don't hesitate to experiment with a rapid retrieve when all else fails. Small minnows are their favorite natural bait, either fished on a leadhead jig or still-fished with a bobber.

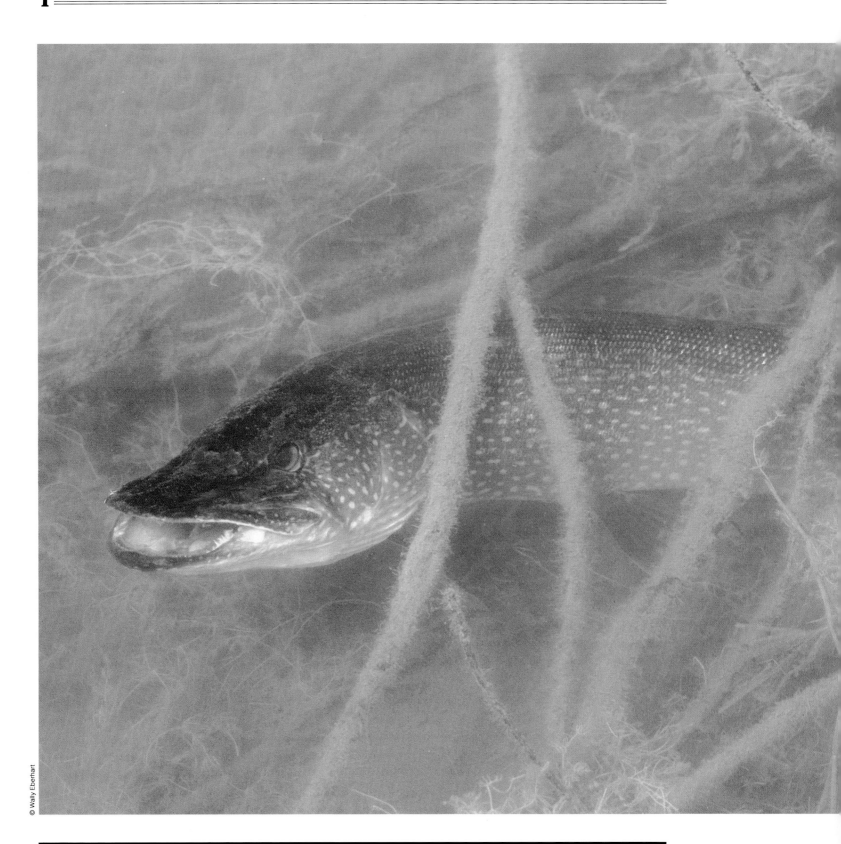

© Wally Eberhart

Northern pike typically lurk hidden in weedbeds, waiting to dart out and seize a minnow or passing lure.

"You're casting too hard," he finally offered. "Here," he said, "use my other rod. It's a softer action, and you'll be more gentle in your casting. Easy does it'll put you right on the fish."

I never did match Slider's numbers, but my own score did increase substantially that afternoon and other days as a result of his advice.

Bait-casting rods vary widely in length, action, and proper lure weight, and are classified as either ultralight, light, medium, or heavy. These classifications are based on the appropriate lure weights (and corresponding line weights) for each. Ultralight bait-casting rods are designed for ⅛- to ¼- ounce (3.5- to 7-g) lures. These might be used with 4-, 6- or even 8-pound- (1.8-, 2.7-, 3.6-g-) test line, and should be of a soft action for use with very light lures. When using such light line on bait-casting reels, you'll need to be very careful to keep the line from slipping between the spool's edge and the reel frame. Since spin-casting reels work best with relatively light lines, ultralight bait-casting rods are usually good spin-casting rods and work well for sunfish,

perch, crappies, smallmouth bass, open-water walleye, and even stream and pond trout.

Light bait-casting rods are usually used with lines testing at 6 to 10 pounds (2.7 to 4.5 kg) and lure weights of ¼ to ⅜ ounces (7 to 10.5 g) or slightly more. In many areas, this is the all-around outfit for large- and smallmouth bass, walleye, and pike in open water. In the summer, many bass lakes see parades of anglers, swimmers, and water skiers all day long, so using small lures and light lines can often be the only way to take even large bass. Light bait-casting rigs can be ideal for such fishing.

Medium bait-casting rods accommodate lure weights from ⅜ to ⅝ ounces (10.5 to 17.5 g) using 10- to 20-pound- (4.5- to 9-g-) test line. Such rods may be either single- or two-handed, and are commonly used for large fish and in snag-filled water. In many situations these rods may be ideal for largemouth bass, northern pike, lake trout, and even muskellunge if smaller muskie baits are used. There are very few spin-casting reels calibered for lines and lures this heavy, so most spin-casters use ultralight or light rods.

Heavy bait-casting rods are almost always two-handed, and carry lures of ¾ to 1¼ ounces (21 to 35 g) or more. These are commonly used for heavy trolling, casting for muskellunge or lake trout, and for salmon or steelhead fishing. Heavy bait-casting rods are most often used in salt water.

The important thing in putting together an outfit is not to look for a line that will sail across the Missouri or a rod that will toss a lead sinker over the post office, but a modest set of tools designed to baffle a trout lying in plain sight.

—A. J. McClane

Chapter 7
Fly Rods

As with most rods, each fly rod is designed to throw a specific weight. Since artificial flies are virtually weightless, the weight being thrown is that of the bulky line, which is cast in a long, unrolling loop to deliver the fly. A further difference is that the casting weight—the line—isn't measured in ounces but rather according to a standardized system adopted by the American Fishing Tackle Manufacturer's Association (AFTMA) in 1961 that designates fly-line sizes from 1 through 14, with 14 being heaviest. Thus fly rods are referred to as a 1-weight or a 6-weight and so forth, depending on the size line the particular rod is designed to cast.

With fly rods, the designated line weight is almost completely independent of rod length, and depends mostly on a particular manufacturer's design. For example, one rod-maker may offer a 6-foot (1.8-m), 4-weight rod for fishing nymphs on a small brushy trout creek and also sell a 9-foot (2.7-m), 4-weight rod for small dry flies on a larger trout river. The very same maker may also sell a 9-foot (2.7-m), 14-weight whose apparent stoutness would make it most appropriate for ocean-going marlin. For most freshwater fishing, the most common fly rods are from 7 to 9 feet (2.1 to 2.7 m) long, and take lines from a super delicate 3-weight to a robust 9-weight that might be used for jumbo largemouth bass.

Most beginning fly anglers fish in areas where they'll be fishing for either trout or bass or both, and maybe a few panfish such as bluegills. The best fly rod for a beginner is an 8½- to 9-foot (2.5- to 2.7-m) rod that takes 6-weight line. This rod is light enough for even a bluegill battle to assume a little

Courtesy G·Loomis/inset photo © Christopher Bain

Most makers offer a wide range of fly rod models, of which these are a few examples.

Courtesy Orvis Company, Inc.

This lightweight rod features a light, sliding-ring reelseat.

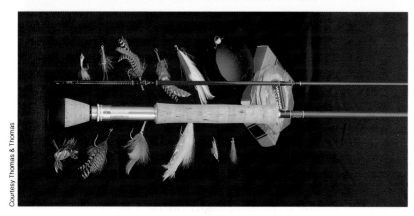

Courtesy Thomas & Thomas

This heavy-duty fly rod and the large saltwater flies pictured would be a good combination for pike.

drama, and also can be used successfully for both steelhead and Atlantic salmon. Many people make the mistake of starting a beginner with a rod of less than 7 feet (2.1 m), believing the shorter rod will be easier for a youngster or novice to handle. In fact, shorter rods put a premium on the caster's timing and often can be frustrating, good intentions not withstanding.

It is essential that the fly-casting outfit be balanced; that is, the line used must match the line size the rod is designed for. The only exception is in the case of a novice who's having trouble getting the feel of the line in the air while casting. In this case, it may be advisable to use a line one size larger, which will effectively overload the rod and provide a greater feel. After the novice gains some casting proficiency, he or she can switch back to the correct line. Most major fly-tackle makers offer balanced outfits that include a matched rod, reel, and line at the very least. These outfits are usually less expensive than purchasing the individual components separately.

Most premium fly-rod grips are made of glued and shaped cork rings, and a reelseat that is located behind the grip. The reel is usually fastened with a threaded ring to the reelseat, although some light rods have sliding bands. There may be a small hook-keeper ring located on the rod butt just forward of the grip; this is for storing your fly and is not a line guide, although many first-timers make the mistake of stringing their line here. The larger and first guide on the butt section is the stripping guide; it is this guide that gets the most wear as you strip or reel in line, so check to make sure it isn't cracked or rough in any way. The remainder of the guides are usually snake guides, so called because of their twisted-wire design. The last, or tip, guide is usually pear-shaped and may feature a ceramic insert.

Most fly rods are of at least a two-piece design, and some may even be three, four, or more pieces to make storage and travel easier. In these cases, ferrules are usually of the sleeve or spigot variety. Sleeve-type ferrules are assembled by fitting one end of a section over the end of the preceding section. If the ferrules get stuck, they can be gently twisted loose. Spigot ferrules rely on a round tube that fits inside the mating sections and is permanently fixed inside one of them. Unlike sleeve-type ferrules, spigot ferrules can be easily damaged by twisting and should be parted with a straight pull only. In either case, keep your ferrules wiped clean and lightly lubricate them with paraffin if necessary.

To go beyond the beginner's outfit described earlier in this chapter, you'll need to know how to match your rod/line size to the types of fish you're trying to catch. Just as a rod is most effective when casting a certain size line, the rod/line combination is most effective when casting flies of a certain size. A large, air-resistant bass bug, for example, is very hard to cast on a delicate 4-weight outfit

*These medium-weight fly rods
are suitable for most trout
fishing as well as small bass
and panfish.*

because the line's mass is insufficient to carry the big bug through the air. And while you could cast a small trout fly with a 9-weight bass outfit, you'd lose the delicate touch that makes trout fishing fun.

Lightweight rods, 3- and 4-weight, are suitable for trout flies size 10 and smaller as well as small bugs suitable for panfish. These light-line rods work most easily in situations where there is little wind. If you're consistently fishing with small flies, these are definitely the rods of choice.

Medium-weight rods, 5-, 6-, and 7-weight, are the most versatile. Five-weights are sufficiently delicate for small flies, yet can also handle small bass bugs. Six- and 7-weights are slightly more versatile than 5-weight; using them means a sacrifice of a little delicacy, but a gain in flexibility. They can be cast with medium-size bass bugs, as well as salmon and steelhead flies and contain enough internal strength to help an experienced angler handle these high-jumping, long-running fish.

Heavy-weight rods, 8- and 9-weight, are used for large flies and fish. These are well suited for bass-bugging, since large bugs are most easily cast with these heavier lines. These sizes can also be used for steelhead and for Atlantic salmon. Long casts are the rule in steelhead and salmon fishing, so the heavy lines are a help in this regard. In general, these are powerful, big-fish rods that also see considerable use for saltwater fishing.

Courtesy Orvis Company, Inc.

Trout in many Western creeks
are partial to small flies,
requiring delicacy of both fly
rod and fisherman.

*Most premium fly rods such as
this one are now made from
synthetic graphite fibers that
offer an optimum combination
of light weight and strength.*

The act of fly-casting itself seems simple,
yet it requires hours of practice for reasonable proficiency. Teaching fly-casting is beyond the scope of this book, but here are a
few suggestions. There's no substitute for personal instruction to get you started. First, see
if you can find a fly-fishing friend to teach
you. You might also consider attending one
of the many fly-fishing schools held by both
manufacturers and professional casting teach-
ers. You can locate a school by checking the
advertisements in one of several fly-fishing
magazines you'll find on most good news-
stands. Fly-casting videotapes are available,
as are books on the subject. Two highly rec-
ommended books, both by excellent teach-
ers, are: *Fly-Casting Techniques* by Joan Wulff
(New York: Nick Lyons Books, 1987); and *The
Essence of Flycasting* by Mel Krieger (write
to: Club Pacific, 790 27th Avenue, San Fran-
cisco, CA 94121).

NORTHERN PIKE

Some refer to the northern pike as the water wolf, perhaps from its habit of taking an occasional duckling from the reed-studded surface of a lake. Northern pike, however, feed mostly on yellow perch, suckers, and other easily caught forage fishes. Pike will rest almost unseen in weedbeds at various depths, from which they'll explode in a vicious rush to grab their prey or a lure. Pike are not long-running fish, but will bulldog against a line and often make dramatic leaps when trying to throw a lure. They sometimes come easily to the side of the boat, at which point you should beware of the violent trashing that invariably follows at that precise moment.

Pike are common to cool-water lakes and some rivers in the northern United States and Canada.

They've been recorded at well over 40 pounds (18-kg), but today a 20-pounder (9-kg) is a big one, even in wilderness Canadian waters where 30-pounders (13.5-kg) are possible. Pike in the 4- to 12-pound (1.8- to 5.4-kg) range are common in many areas.

Pike are great sport on medium-weight spinning or bait-casting tackle, and some specialists go after them with heavy fly tackle as well. A wire leader is customary because the fish has such sharp teeth. Flashy spoons and larger bass lures are usually good for pike, as are big, colorful streamer flies tied on 3/0 hooks. The secret to catching these wily fish is usually an erratic retrieve that will tease them into striking, which works much better than a steady reeling.

PART III
LURES and FLIES

Bits of wood, plastic, metal, and feathers are parts of the lure maker's palette, combined in seemingly endless variations as the plugs, spinners, and flies that fill our tackleboxes. Each of these lures is designed to be used in a particular situation. The wobbling spoon that takes pickerel in a weedy cove may have to be switched for a deep-diving plug to take smallmouths over a nearby reef. A surface plug may suffice to tempt largemouths along the evening shoreline, but a yellow jig may be necessary for walleye where the water suddenly deepens. There then, is the angler's perpetual problem—trying to decide which lures to select among the hundreds and hundreds of different ones that brighten the walls of any well-stocked tackle shop.

If one type of lure worked well all the time, there certainly would be little reason for the myriad choices. But all fish—from the smallest sunfish to the largest steelhead—can be exceptionally fussy, and the thoughtfully well-stocked tacklebox is essential for consistent fishing success.

The same questions pertain to fly fishing, of course, where there are more than twenty thousand recognized fly patterns and where even the selection at a local fly shop may amount to several hundred different flies. At any given time, however, only a few of them will work. Whether you are plugging for bass or fly fishing for trout, picking the right lure or fly is much more than simple guesswork, as you'll see in the following chapters.

Poor Isaac Walton! Little did he think, when moving along by the banks and rivers of Staffordshire, with his cumbrous equipments, that any unworthy disciple of his would ever be so gorgeously fitted out, with all that art and taste can accomplish for the pursuit of his favorite sport!

—Daniel Webster

Chapter 8
Spoons and Spinners

Julio Buehl was enjoying a country picnic in the grand Victorian manner until he accidentally dropped a piece of silverware over the side of the boat upon which he was lunching. He watched as the silver spoon fluttered on the surface, then twisted down into the depths of water. Buehl gasped as he observed a huge northern pike slash suddenly at the flashing metal. Buehl forgot about his lunch as he hurriedly rowed ashore, then ran to the back shed on his farm where he kept his tools. There he quickly hacked the handles off half a dozen spoons, drilled holes in their ends, then hammered shut the eyes of hooks around the holes. He returned to the lake, and used the first spoon lure to catch a brace of pike.

The turn-of-the-century invention of the spoon is one of the most pervasive bits of angling folklore. Of course, the spoon may not have been invented exactly this way, but the anecdote is a convincing one. In any case, soon thereafter spoons became and remain one of the most widely used types of lure. You can, by the way, make a spoon-type lure using an actual spoon, but this shape tends to spin in the water and will generate line twist, unlike the modern spoon that at normal retrieving speeds wobbles back and forth over its long axis without actually revolving.

SPOONS

Within the confines of a general teardrop shape, there are spoons of every size and

An assortment of spoons. The smallest versions are best for trout and panfish while the largest will work for lake trout or pike.

color imaginable. Modern spoons fall in three categories, however: casting, jigging, and trolling. A single spoon could be used for all three, of course, but some design modifications made for each of these three categories help narrow down the choices.

Casting spoons are the most commonly used, and are relatively thick in proportion to their length, while they retain enough surface area to provide a wobbling action when retrieved. If a spoon is to be cast, its weight should be concentrated in the rear to a certain extent, which will retard tumbling when the lure is cast. Regular Daredevles, Krocodiles, and Little Cleos are examples of such lures.

Jigging spoons are extremely dense or thick in proportion to their size. Their weight is concentrated at the end of the lure. Vertical deep jigging is commonly done with these lures, as their weight allows them to sink rapidly to the desired depth while it gives them an attractive flutter when twitched up and down. Hopkins spoons and Kastmasters are two examples of popular jigging spoons.

Trolling spoons tend to be much lighter in proportion to their overall size. They are difficult to cast, but their relative lightness means a sharper, more abrupt flutter when dragged through the water; this increased action can pay off in more fish for the persistent troller. The Northport Nailer may be the best-known spoon of this type.

As the previous descriptions show, the thicker the spoon in proportion to its area, the deeper it will fish—that's what you should consider when choosing a spoon. No spoon will work any better than the angler retrieving it, however, and retrieving is the real art of fishing with lures. It's critical that you be able to vary your retrieve, so here are a few options. The first is to simply reel in your spoon at a moderate pace, with the hope that the spoon's inherent wobbling action will entice your bass or trout. If this doesn't work, it's better first to change tactics instead of changing lures. Try casting and alternating quick turns of the reel handle with slow ones, which will cause the spoon to erratically wobble and dart in the water. You can also accentuate this action with short sweeps of your rod tip; in fact, this is much more representative of a bait fish struggling to escape and is a very successful approach. On other days, a hyperactive, fast retrieve may pull fish when nothing else works. The key is to experiment until you find something that works: Remember that the biggest difference between novice and expert anglers is that the expert is willing and able to vary retrieves.

Spoons are the closest things we have to universal lures. Thumbnail-size spoons are used with fly- and ultralight-spinning gear for panfish and spooky trout. Other versions in the ⅛- to ⅜-ounce (3.5- to 10.5-g) range are

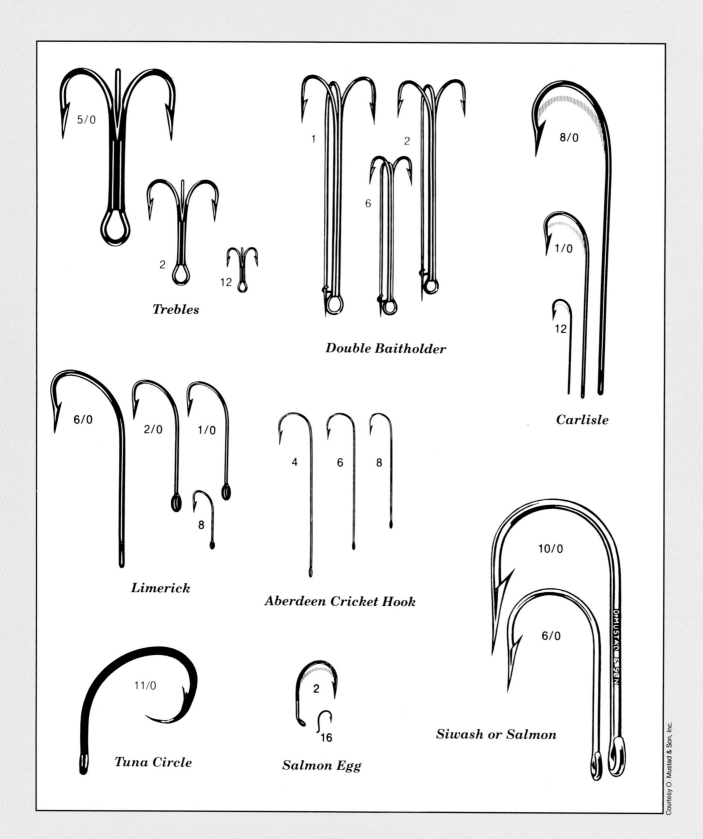

5/0
2
12

Trebles

1
6
2

Double Baitholder

8/0
1/0
12

Carlisle

6/0
2/0
1/0
8

Limerick

4
6
8

Aberdeen Cricket Hook

10/0
6/0

Siwash or Salmon

11/0

Tuna Circle

2
16

Salmon Egg

UNDERSTANDING HOOK SIZES

Hook sizes are often a confounding question for novice anglers since the size numbers bear no relation to the actual size of a hook. The numbering system is archaic, but now is just a matter of convention. Here's a simple way to keep track of what's what among hook sizes.

First, remember that a size 1 hook is the center point of a size scale. Hook sizes 2, 4, 6, 8, and so on to size 28 get smaller as the size number increases, with size 28 being the smallest. There are no odd-numbered sizes (no size 17, for example) in this sequence. Going in the other direction, hook sizes larger than size 1 are noted with a number, a slash, and a zero: 1/0, 2/0, 3/0,

and so on up to giant 20/0 shark hooks. This sequence does include odd-numbered sizes.

All common freshwater hooks follow this system, which applies to both single hooks and to the treble (three-pointed) hooks commonly found on fishing lures. On the opposite page, a few single hooks are shown actual size to give you some idea of relative size scales. In terms of usage, hooks for artificial flies usually range from a size 2 for large bass flies to size 28 for the very smallest trout flies that are less than ¼ inch (6 mm) long. Bait anglers commonly use hook sizes 2, 4, 6, and 8, and follow the general rule of using smaller hooks for smaller fish and vice versa.

Courtesy Eppinger Mfg. Company

cast for everything from bass, walleye, and trout to big steelhead and salmon. Still larger spoons, from ½ to more than 2 ounces (14 to more than 56 g) are cast or trolled for lake trout, northern pike, and muskellunge. Once you've determined the action and size of the spoons you need, be sure to have a good selection of available colors to appeal to the whims of the fish.

SPINNERS

Spinners are based on the principle of a flat blade being spun around a central shaft by either a water current or the pressure of the water on the blade when the lure is retrieved in still water. The rotating blade offers the flash, movement, and vibration or noise that game fish find so attractive.

Because the blade itself is largely the basis for the spinner's action and effectiveness, spin-

These are typical spinners suited for everything from trout to big muskies.

ners vary largely by blade shape. A nearly round or elliptical blade pattern offers the greatest water resistance, and thus will spin in a slow current or with a slow retrieve. Colorado-style blades are examples of this type. Additionally, Indiana-style blades are somewhat more elliptical and require a little more water pressure (meaning a faster retrieve) to spin. Long slender willowleaf-style blades are the opposite extreme; their slenderness requires the fastest retrieve for the necessary action. Given this information, you can readily scan a selection of spinners and accurately predict how each type will need to be fished.

Courtesy Luhr-Jensen

Smaller spoons, spinners, and plugs are best used with light-weight spinning tackle.

Red-and-white Daredevle spoons (above right) are the all-time classic lures of this type.

Larger spoons are excellent lake-trout lures when trolled very slowly, usually near the bottom of a lake.

Courtesy Eppinger Mfg. Company

Courtesy Eppinger Mfg. Company

Most blades are attached to a central wire shaft with a clevis or U-shaped fixture that allows the blade to revolve. Brass beads or similar devices are usually located on the shaft below the clevis and blade to add casting and fishing weight. Coupled with the inherent blade shape, this weight determines how deeply the spinner will run at a given retrieve speed. A heavy spinner with a large round blade will thus run slowly and deeply, and might be a good walleye lure. A lighter version with a willowleaf blade could be retrieved quickly near the surface where its speed and action are appropriate for pike.

Some spinners have their treble hook decorated with feathers or brightly dyed squirrel or deer-tail hair. Those decorated with hair may be called bucktails in reference to the larger sizes used commonly for muskellunge. Because of their constant rotation, spinners are seldom used for trolling because they will twist your line. You should try to avoid this problem, even in casting by using a first-quality snap swivel ahead of the lure.

Like spoons, spinners come in a wide range of sizes, from tiny $1/_{32}$-ounce (.9-g) models that are ideal for bluegills, perch, and crappies to 1-ounce (28-g) and larger models for heavy-duty muskellunge fishing. Of course, the spinner sizes you select should match the rest of your tackle. Retrieves can likewise be varied, although the extent of the variation isn't as great as with spoons. Still, a mixed retrieve of fast and slow reeling will usually produce more fish than a steady cranking.

© Wally Eberhart

Walleyes have large, sharp front teeth, so be careful in landing and releasing them.

Courtesy Luhr-Jensen

The two spinners (left) and thick spoons (right) will run deep, while the larger spoon (center) is a thin trolling model.

SPINNERBAITS AND BUZZBAITS

Spinnerbaits and buzzbaits are modern variations of spinners, and have come into wide use for bass and pike fishing. Spinnerbaits have one, or sometimes two, spinner blades in tandem on one fork of a V-shaped wire shaft. The lower shaft is terminated by a lead head and hook, and is usually decorated by a rubber skirt or similar device. The vibration of the upper spinner wiggles the lead-head's skirt when retrieved—the effect on largemouth bass can be devastating. Because of the added weight, the spinner blades also spin when the lure is simply sinking; this is often when a bass or pike grabs the lure, so you'll have to be alert.

Buzzbaits depend essentially on a large spinner directly in front of a bucktail or similar lure body. The oversize blade buzzes and clatters near or at the surface when retrieved, usually at high speed. The commotion is sometimes more than a poor bass can resist.

Buzzbaits are especially effective in bass lakes where there are a lot of dead treetops showing above the water's surface. You might want to try casting beyond the logical bass hiding places near the standing timber, then retrieving the lure closely past the bass's doorstep, adjacent to the trees. Buzzbaits also work well in weedy areas where pike may be concentrated because the lure runs near the surface, which usually prevents tangling in the weeds.

The endless variety of plugs makes the subject confusing and complicated and even controversial if not treated with care.

— **Ray Bergman**

Chapter 9
Plugs

If you're handy with a jackknife, it's possible to whittle a respectable bass lure from a chunk of light cedar and, with the addition of some hooks and a little paint, get right down to the business of fishing. That's how bass plugs were made before they started to be widely manufactured after World War I; they were sometimes made from the round, wooden bung or "plug" from a common barrel. These lures have come a long way since James Heddon started making his Dowagiac Minnows in the early days of midwestern bass fishing. They are now available in a wide range of sizes; there are small plugs for trout and panfish to giant plugs that would scare the fins off all but the most aggressive muskellunge. Their names have changed somewhat, too. Since some plugs resemble bait, many people refer to them as "baits," and since they're cast and retrieved, the term "crankbait" has replaced plug in the lexicon of many bass anglers.

Modern plugs fall into one of several categories, which, as with other lures, can help you determine how and when to use a particular type. These categories are not based on size or weight, but on how the plugs are designed to perform in or on the water. In all cases the relative success of a particular plug depends as much on the angler's manipulation as on the plug's design. In general, the categories are: poppers, skimmers, floater-divers, and deep-divers.

POPPING PLUGS

Popping plugs are floating surface plugs that have a cupped or concave face to disturb the surface and thus attract a fish's attention. They

The J-plug on top is commonly used for trolling because its multiple-hook rigging will tangle when cast. The lower plug is designed for casting or trolling and has a long lip to force it deep under the water's surface when retrieved.

Courtesy Luhr-Jensen

are most commonly used for largemouth bass, although in smaller sizes are equally suitable for smallmouths. Some versions may be decorated with a rubber skirt, or feature jointed bodies for added action. Sizes range from tiny ⅛-ounce (3.5-g) and even smaller versions for fly-casting or ultralight spinning to poppers of 1 ounce (28 g) or more for muskies and pike. Even larger versions are used in saltwater fishing. You will find that the most common bass-fishing sizes are ¼, ⅜, ½, and ⅝ ounces (7, 10.5, 14, and 17.5 g).

Poppers should generally be worked slowly. If bass fishing, allow the ripples from the plug's splashdown to disappear before you begin working the plug. Although a loud pop and gurgle might attract fish from a good distance, it might also scare fish in the immediate vicinity. Work the plug very gently at first. If no fish is forthcoming, try a louder pop and gurgle by twitching the rod tip harder, but remember to let the plug sit still for as much as thirty seconds between pops. Also keep your rod tip low so you can set the hook with a hard sweep of the rod when a bass slams your plug. Although a rapid, gurgling, popping retrieve will sometimes take bass— especially if they're chasing schools of

baitfish – the usual rule is the slower the retrieve the better. Poppers work best in early morning and late evening along a lake or river shoreline, in lily-pad coves, and off points— all of these are places where bass come to feed in the shallows.

SKIMMING PLUGS

Skimmers are surface-disturbing plugs that are available in a wide variety of styles. Some, like the famous Jitterbug or Crazy Crawler, have a face plate or metal arms that make the lure wobble and gurgle when retrieved. Others may be cigar-shaped with small propellers in the front and back of the lure that churn the surface when the plug is twitched. And others, like the old Zara Spook, have no such devices and depend on the angler's rod manipulations for an attractive action. A few ultralight versions of these lures are available, but most skimmers are available in the same sizes as standard bass-fishing lures, from ¼ to ⅝ ounces (7 to 17.5 g).

Courtesy Luhr-Jensen (all photos)

An assortment of colors is essential when you buy a selection of plugs to accommodate the variable whims of fish.

The sharp lip on this plug will cause it to dive and wobble when retrieved.

This Hot Shot plug has an extended lip for deep-diving action.

Like poppers, skimmers are used mostly for bass and usually work best when fished slowly. In fact, with all varieties, it's wise to let them lie on the water until the disturbance their landing causes disappears. Wobbling-type plugs work well with an intermittent retrieve: reel the plug toward you for 2 or 3 feet (.6 or .9 m), let it sit, then reel again. Propeller-type plugs benefit from the same type of intermittent action, but are best worked with twitches and sweeps of the rod tip rather than simple reeling. It's also worth trying an ultrafast retrieve with these plugs if bass are chasing baitfish. In fact, unadorned plugs such as the Zara are sometimes the most deadly lures of all. These plugs should sit motionless on the water for as much as a minute, then be given the smallest possible twitch, then allowed to sit still again. The long pauses allow curious bass to come investigate. The little twitches can even cause one to mistake your plug for a crippled minnow and blast into it.

FLOATING-DIVING PLUGS

Floating-diving plugs are the most diverse and versatile group of plugs. There are minnow-shaped swimmers such as Rapalas

© Tony Cenicola/lure by Heddon

The Crazy Crawler is a classic surface plug for bass. The two metal arms cause the plug to wobble and gurgle along the water's surface, which can drive the bass nuts.

This large walleye took a shallow-running crankbait, a good bet for walleyes at dawn and dusk when these shy fish frequent the shallows.

or Rebels. There are also fatter plugs that simulate crayfish or deep-bodied shad (both favorite bass foods). In either case, floating-diving lures have a metal or plastic lip on the front that makes them dive under the surface and wobble when retrieved. In ultrasmall sizes (less than ⅛ ounce [3.5 g]), these lures are terrific for trout and panfish in addition to bass. Slightly larger versions can be good for walleye—especially after dark—and some are even designed especially for steelhead and Pacific salmon. Bigger versions are used for muskies and pike.

Once again, a slightly erratic retrieve is the secret to using these plugs. After you cast, allow the plug to sit and then give it a twitch with your rod tip to make it dive under the surface and then float back up. (This is my favorite black-bass technique. It can drive the fish crazy.) You can also rapidly reel the lure in, stop it, then move it quickly again. This retrieve will cause the lure to dart through the water like a living creature. Another method is to reel as fast as you can to simulate a minnow or crayfish trying to escape a predatory bass or walleye. This action will take the lure to its maximum running depth of 3 to 7 feet (.9 to 2.1 m), and can be one way to work a sloping shoreline either by boat or from shore.

DEEP-DIVING PLUGS

Deep-diving plugs are typically floating plugs with an extra-large lip on the front that causes them to plane down to as much as 30 feet (9 m) when retrieved or trolled. When bass or walleye are holding deep over weedbeds, rocks, or other bottom structure, these are the plugs to use. Sinking plugs should also be included in this category. These may have a smaller lip or wobbling surface, but because they sink they can reach a considerable depth before being retrieved.

Finally, plug colors vary widely, but it's better to start with imitative colors, the old standbys such as frog, perch, and silver. Yellow is often good, too, yet there will be days when the local smallmouths will eat anything that is bright chartreuse. Many experts like an all-black finish on surface plugs for bass fishing after dark. Remember, though, that fish seldom follow any rules as to plug color (or anything else), so experimenting with plug color at any given time could be helpful.

SMALLMOUTH BASS

Smallmouth bass are "pound for pound, the gamest fish that swims," according to the late Dr. James Henshall, an American bass-fishing pioneer. Millions of anglers may well agree, as this fish seems second in popularity only to its largemouth cousin. Smallmouths prefer clear, rocky lakes and are found in many more rivers than largemouths, which tend to avoid currents. Smallmouths will leap higher, run longer, generally fight more frantically than largemouths, and, consequently, deserve every inch of their hard-fighting reputation among anglers.

Smallmouth bass may reach 12 pounds (5.4 kg) or even more, but bass this large are very rare. The average catch is 10 to 15 inches (25 to 37.5 cm) long and weighs up to 2 or 3 pounds (.9 or 1.35 kg) in both rivers and lakes.

Smallmouths are wary, but happily are found in relatively open water that permits the use of light tackle and lures. Fly anglers often use bass bugs—the slider-type preferred over noisier poppers. Bright yellow and black are good lure colors. Spin- and bait-casters can score with the usual variety of bass lures in smaller sizes, but the best bet in most waters is a 3-inch (7.5-cm) curly-tail plastic grub on a ⅛-ounce (3.5-g) leadhead jig. Dawn and dusk are usually the best times to fish for smallmouths on both lakes and rivers.

A visit to a first-class fishing-tackle shop is more interesting than an afternoon at the circus.

— Theodore Gordon

Chapter 10
Plastic Baits and Jigs

With the growth of vinyl-resin technology during the 1930s and 1940s came soft plastic lures of every description. Their acceptance by both anglers and fish has come mostly in bass fishing. Today the plastic worm is the most popular plastic bait for bass. It's essential in every tacklebox.

Plastic worms are available in a wide range of sizes and colors. Many also have additional features to attract fish such as scents, flavors, special textures, built-in rattles, and noisemakers. Most are thicker toward the head. The thinner tail has molded curves that make it undulate and wiggle when the lure is sinking or is drawn through the water. The most popular version—and that with which you should start—is a 6-inch- (15-cm-) long, translucent purple or "grape" worm.

Plastic worms come unadorned with hooks or spinners and can be rigged in a variety of ways, depending on how you're going to fish them. Common to most methods is a large worm hook designed for fishing with plastic bait (not used for fishing with real worms). Most of these hooks have a bend or offset near the eye that allows the worm to be rigged and remain straight. Worm hooks must be ultrasharp since they must penetrate both the worm and the bass's hard mouth on the strike.

The first method of fishing a plastic worm is fishing it on or near the surface without additional weight. Using a Trilene Knot (page 123), tie the worm hook on your line without a swivel snap. Insert the hook point through the worm's head to a distance equal to the length of the offset near the hook eye. Pull

Most plastic baits, including these small fish, are very flexible and feature a molded tail or curl for added action in the water.

Courtesy Mister Twister

(4.5-kg-) test monofilament on a medium-weight outfit, but should go to lighter line if you're not fishing in weeds or other cover. Cast the worm to an opening or pocket in the lily pads, or an area where it will sink very slowly. Making its tail wiggle, twitch the worm gently near the surface, then rest. Twitch again and rest to give the bass plenty of time to study the lure. Strikes, when they come, may be no more than a gentle pull, at other times a violent swirl. You'll need to set the hook hard, so make sure your rod tip is low in anticipation of a strike; this should give you plenty of room for a powerful upward sweep.

The second method simply involves rigging the worm in the same manner and adding one or two lead split-shot on the line ahead of the worm to give both added depth and casting weight. The first split-shot should be 1 or 2 feet (30 or 60 cm) above the worm, and the second split-shot at least 1 foot (30 cm) above the first. By spreading the weights in this fashion, you'll avoid tangling when you cast. Now you can simply cast the worm to wherever you think a bass may be and reel in the worm *slowly*, relying on the worm's built-in action to pull the fish.

The third and final method allows fishing in the deeper waters that many walleye, as well as largemouth and smallmouth bass seem to prefer in the summer. Rig the worm as previously described, but before tying on the hook, thread the line through the hole in the

the hook most of the way through the worm so the offset, hookeye, and knot are buried in the worm's head. Rotate the worm on the hook, then insert the hook point so that the point and barb are buried in the worm and that the hook point is *not* sticking out the other side. By covering the hook point, you can make your rig virtually weedless. The worm should lie more or less straight after the hook has been inserted properly.

Because the worm is lightweight, you should use a spinning rod when fishing it. You can get adequate castability with 10-pound-

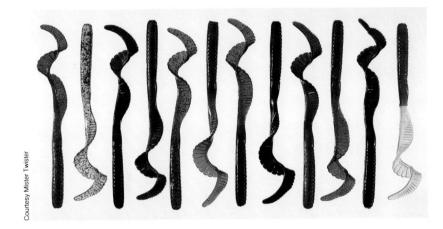

Courtesy Mister Twister

Plastic worms are available in a rainbow of colors, all of which sometimes work. The basic colors, however, are purple or black.

middle of a bullet-shaped, lead worm weight so the thick end of the weight is toward the end of the line. Now, tie on the hook and rig the worm. Next, slide the weight down the line so it rests on the head of the worm. To hold the weight in position, jam a wooden toothpick hard into the front of the hole in the weight where the line comes out. Snap off the remainder of the toothpick, and the weight is securely in place. Some bass anglers call this a Texas-style rig, based on the area where it supposedly originated.

The size of the weight will govern how fast the worm will sink and the depth at which you will fish. Weights generally range from ⅛ ounce (3.5 g) to as much as ½ ounce (14 g) or more for very deep jigging. Cast the worm in likely bass cover, or over a deep reef, and let it sink. Pay close attention since many bass will hit as the worm sinks. If nothing happens, retrieve the worm with a gentle up-and-down jigging motion; set the hook hard if you feel the smallest tap or bump.

The other most useful plastic bait is a short, soft curly-tailed grub. These are generally 2 to 4 inches (5 to 10 cm) long with a thick head and a molded curl in the thin tail that makes it vibrate rapidly when jigged or retrieved. Grubs are usually used by themselves

on a leadhead jig in the 1/16- to ¼-ounce (1.75- to 7-g) range, and are sometimes added to the large hook of a spinnerbait or rubber-skirted jig as a trailer to provide additional action. The smaller sizes are terrific for perch and other panfish and will even work for trout at times. The larger sizes, 3- or 4-inch (7.5- or 10-cm) grubs on ⅛-ounce (3.5-g) or heavier leadheads, are terrific for both large- and smallmouth bass and walleye.

Grubs are versatile and easy to use. Tie on a bare leadhead jig with a Trilene Knot (page 123) and no snap swivel. Insert the hook point at the head of the grub and thread the hook through as you push the grub on to, and covering the hook shank behind, the leadhead. This lure can simply be cast and retrieved at a moderate pace, but varying your retrieve is invariably more effective. The same lure can be fished in deep water by allowing it to sink and then retrieving it with a gentle jigging motion. Grubs are a favorite smallmouth-bass lure, for which you might use a ⅛-ounce (3.5-g) leadhead with a 3-inch (7.5-cm) grub on a light spinning rod and 4- or 6-pound- (1.8- or 2.7-g-) test line. The best colors are, in order, clear chartreuse, black, and white.

There's a myriad of other plastic lures of almost every description imitating, among other things, lizards, frogs, minnows, crayfish, eels, and assorted insect larvae. All of these lures have their place and time, but it's the angler—not the lure—who catches the fish.

It is just as well to remember that angling is only a recreation, not a profession. We usually find that men of the greatest experience are the most liberal and least dogmatic... It is often the man of limited experience who is most confident.

— **Theodore Gordon**

Chapter 11
Artificial Flies

Artificial flies have been in use for over two thousand years. The concept of an artificial fly is simple: If a fish is eating insects, you can buy or make something on a hook that resembles that particular insect and use it to fool the fish. In addition, natural flies are generally too small and fragile to be used as bait. Early artificial flies were made with bits of wool and feathers on a primitive hook. Now, flies vary in size, color, form, and function, as determined by how the feathers, fur, and other components are assembled on the hook. Each specific combination is called a "pattern," and there are literally thousands of fly patterns available for every freshwater fish that will take a lure.

Flies are grouped by category and by the types of fish they're designed to catch, which helps to narrow down the choices considerably. First, there are dry flies, which are fished on the water's surface, and wet flies, which are fished just below the surface. Trout dry flies are generally small, within the size 10 to 28 range, while dry flies for Atlantic salmon or steelhead may be as small as size 16 but are commonly size 8 or larger. Dry flies for large- and smallmouth bass, usually called bass bugs, may be colorful affairs of cork, feathers, and other materials on special hooks with a wide opening or gap to facilitate hooking the fish. Smaller versions are often used for bluegills and other panfish that share the bass's habitat.

Wet flies are a more diverse category than dry flies. Simple wet flies for trout have soft-fibered feathers or "hackle" of various colors

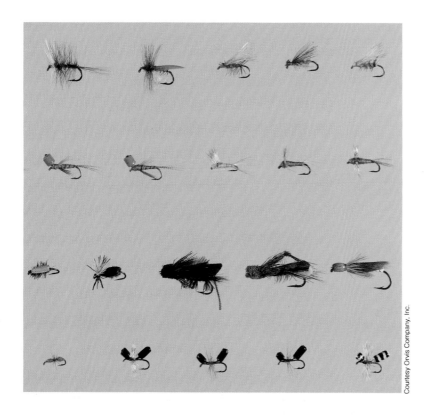

Courtesy Orvis Company, Inc.

Modern dry flies come in a wide array of patterns and sizes.

that fold back over a body. Some wet flies have the addition of wings along the top of the body. Salmon and steelhead wet flies follow the same general design as trout flies, but are usually larger and more colorful. Both trout and salmon flies may be used for bass and panfish; smaller wet flies are especially effective for pond bluegills and smallmouth bass in rivers.

Bucktails and streamers are wet flies that are long, slim, and specifically designed to look like minnows and forage fish. These work well for almost all species of freshwater game fish. Bluegill sunfish will take them in smaller sizes, while sizes 4 through 10 are commonly used for trout and smallmouth bass. Bigger sizes can be used for largemouths, and some huge 1/0 to 3/0 streamers are especially effective for northern pike and even muskellunge.

Nymphs are another type of specialized wet fly, designed to imitate the various larvae of aquatic insects that trout and other fish eat. These flies range from tiny size 20 mayfly nymphs to giant size 4 stonefly nymphs—both are used for trout as circumstances warrant. Nymphs are primarily trout flies, but are also effective for other insect-eating fish from smallmouth bass to bluegill sunfish.

The manner of fishing dry and wet flies is mostly common sense; a wise first step would be to check in the local tackle or fly shop as to what patterns work the best in your area at that particular time. If you see trout rising to a small dark-colored mayfly, it makes little sense to use a big, white dry fly. In almost all cases, it pays to use a fly that closely imitates the size, color, and shape of what the fish happen to be eating. In addition, you'll have to make your fly behave in the same fashion

Courtesy Orvis Company, Inc.

An assortment of floating bass flies or "bugs." Smallmouth bass generally require the smaller sizes.

Courtesy Orvis Company, Inc.

These streamer flies are generally imitative of the small fish on which larger fish feed.

as the fish's food of the moment in order to be consistently successful. This is a key and often overlooked element in fly fishing.

Dry flies should generally be floated on the water's surface near rising fish. This means casting the fly to a spot upstream from a rising trout and letting the fly float naturally down to the fish. You'll have to avoid drag, which is an unnatural movement of the fly caused by the current's pulling on the attached line. It is sometimes advantageous, however, to twitch the dry fly slightly when it nears the fish to enhance the fly's lifelike appearance. Just be sure the fly floats drag free before and after you make the twitch.

In very clear water, it's common to be able to see a trout coming for a dry fly before the actual strike. This can be tough on your nerves because it's difficult to avoid striking too quickly and pulling the fly away from the fish.

Ed Bromley is a transplanted Englishman who often trout fishes on Letort Spring Creek in Pennsylvania, a stream known for its clear water and wary brown trout. His hair-trigger on the strike was costing him a lot of fish, as he often pulled the fly away too soon, and frightened the fish in the process. He finally hit on a scheme that's become a standard with many other trout anglers: Every time a trout took his fly in a swirl, he said, "God save the Queen!" before lifting his rod in salute to the fish, setting the hook in the process.

He told me that the first few times he tried saying it, he got only as far as "God save..." before yanking on the rod, so he was still missing fish. Eventually, all due deliberation produced the whole phrase, and he was a more successful trout angler.

Wet flies for trout, Atlantic salmon, steelhead, and smallmouth bass are all commonly fished down and across the river's current; usually the fly swings across the current and stops directly below the wading angler. A cast

Courtesy Orvis Company, Inc.

made at right angles to the current will swing around faster than a cast made at a greater downstream angle. Some fish, especially salmon and steelhead, are very fussy about fly speed, so you'll have to experiment. In all cases, the strike may come at any point in the fly swing, but is most likely to occur just as the fly comes to a halt below the angler.

Streamers and bucktails should be made to behave like small fish in the water. The best way to learn what this means is to watch the little fish themselves. You'll see minnows darting about, starting and stopping in the water around your lakeside dock or the edge of a river. Work your fly in the current with a similar start-and-stop motion.

Nymphs, which are most commonly used for trout, are often fished either across and downstream or sometimes with a dead drift. This usually means casting upstream or up and across, allowing the fly to tumble back in the same unencumbered fashion as a natural bug drifting free in the current. This is difficult fishing because the strikes are hard to detect,

An assortment of nymphs and wet flies as commonly used for trout or panfish such as bluegills and perch.

Fly-tying is an enjoyable hobby practiced by millions of anglers worldwide.

Courtesy Orvis Company, Inc.

Courtesy Orvis Company, Inc.

Large- and smallmouth bass will avidly strike at a wide variety of fly-rod bugs. Most of the flies in the upper two rows are surface lures, while most of the lower flies are designed to be twitched along subsurface at various depths.

and some anglers add a very small float or strike indicator to the middle of the leader above the fly to make detecting strikes easier.

Successful fishing with fly-rod bass bugs requires mastering some bass psychology. When the bug splats down on the water next to some lily pads, bass will swim over to investigate but often won't take the bug right away. Usually if the bug gurgles and splashes away quickly the bass will loose interest. Let the bug sit still until the ripples from its landing have disappeared. Then twitch the bug very gently and wait again. The secret is usually in fishing the bug almost more slowly than your patience will allow. When the bass can't stand it any longer, it'll let you know— by engulfing your bug with a vicious splash.

LARGEMOUTH BASS

Based on their wide distribution and the vast numbers of bass anglers, largemouth bass are probably one of the most popular game fishes, particularly in North America. Although the world-record fish, taken in Georgia, topped 22 pounds (10 kg), an average catch in most northern bass ponds will be 12 to 16 inches (30 to 40 cm) long, weighing 1 to 3 pounds (.45 to 1.35 kg). A 5- to 7-pound (2.25- to 3.2-kg) fish is considered a real trophy. The Florida subspecies grows substantially larger and has been introduced successfully in southern California.

Of the many variables in bass fishing, the most important concept is what professional bass anglers call "patterning." This means that many, but not all, of the large-mouths in any given lake will be found at similar locations simultaneously, although circumstances and locations may change from day to day. Thus, if you're catching largemouths in 10 feet (3 m) of water off a rocky point, all similar locations should also pay off on that day. Understanding this concept can save you considerable time searching for fish.

All kinds of tackle are suited for largemouths, depending on such variables as cover, fishing depth, and fish size. Perhaps the most basic and versatile lure is a 6-inch (15-cm), purple plastic worm that can be fished at almost any depth with spinning tackle and the addition of an appropriate sinker or weight.

© Wally Eberhart

PART IV
LINES and ACCESSORIES

In this section we'll review the two most neglected aspects of freshwater fishing tackle—line and accessories. Both categories are often taken for granted by anglers and tackle-shop owners who ruefully find sooner or later that just any old thing won't do after all. A little forethought regarding line and accessories can mean the difference between success or failure on a fishing trip.

The examples are numerous. Perhaps you've met the spin-caster who neglected to put on new line with the new season, so lost every pike he or she hooked over three days of an expensive trip, or the bait-caster whose line consistently went into horrible tangles because his or her snap swivel was too small for the size of the trolling spoon. You also may have encountered the fly angler who fished all day over rising trout with the right fly pattern but the wrong leader and went home empty-handed.

By the time you finish reading this section, you will know how to assemble a balanced outfit for whatever freshwater fish you pursue. The word balance is a key word in fishing; it simply cannot be stressed enough that your tackle should match and each of your components should be in proportion to one another.

As you'll see in this section, there are only a few small things you'll need to keep that balance working in your favor.

Chapter 12

Choosing Your Line

Long strands of light gray hair from a horse's tail, preferably a stallion, are what Izaak Walton used for a fishing line in England when his famous book *The Compleat Angler* was first published in 1653. The hairs were braided into a relatively strong line, and tied to the rod tip for fishing—although collecting the hair in the first place may have been more exciting than the fishing.

Both linen and silk were later used for fishing line. For bait-casting and fly fishing, silk was thinly braided for lure-casting or thickly braided for fly-casting. The trouble with these and all other natural-fiber lines was that they rotted if not completely dried after fishing. They were difficult to maintain and a lack of maintenance usually meant a broken and ruined line.

The technological boom that came with World War II brought nylon and Dacron™ to the fore as fishing-line materials. Today, fibers of these materials are standard lines worldwide. Unlike older lines, these synthetic fibers don't rot, and while some care is required, it is for the most part minimal and usually doesn't extend beyond periodically spooling your reel with fresh line. Nylon is used mostly as monofilament spinning and bait-casting line and for fly-fishing leaders. Dacron™ is usually braided as a multifilament line and is used on some bait-casting and trolling reels, as well as for fly-line backing.

Nylon monofilament will degrade and lose its strength through long exposure to sunlight. That's why it's important to put fresh monofilament on your reels every season.

Monofilament is packaged on spools of various sizes and, as you might expect, the bigger the spool, the lower the cost per yard of line. If you have only one reel, you'll probably be able to fill it from a 200- to 300-yard (180- to 270-m) line spool. If you use many different reels, you may want to buy several bulk spools of line every year, each of which may hold several thousand yards of line.

Most fishing line is labeled according to its static breaking strength, or pound-test; its diameter; and the amount of line on the line spool. The pound-test rating is the amount of steady pull needed to break the line and is an indication of the line's strength. Since the line's diameter is what actually determines how much you can fit on your reel spool, this is also important. Many reel makers label their spools as to line capacity, which may be given as either pound-test or diameter, so you need to know both. The portion of the spool label indicating yardage simply tells you if you're buying enough line in the first place. Unfortunately, most makers don't give a manufacturing date for their line, even though nylon can deteriorate over time and under certain conditions of storage. If you can, buy line from a well-stocked rack or shelf, as this usually indicates that the store's inventory has a relatively high turnover.

Different types of nylon have different properties such as relative stiffness or limpness, elasticity, knot strength, rate of water absorption, etc. Most modern lines are alloys of

Most spools of monofilament are labeled as to breaking strength and line diameter, which you'll need to know to match the line to your particular reel.

Courtesy Orvis Company, Inc.

Sinking-tip fly lines allow fishing at intermediate depths in a pond or river.

different types of nylon designed to optimally combine these characteristics for a particular type of fishing. An ultralight spinning enthusiast might look for the limpest and stretchiest line for the greatest ease in casting light lures and shock absorption in fighting fish. At the other extreme, a muskie angler may want the line with the least stretch, which will allow him to set the hooks hard in the powerful jaws of a muskellunge. Many monofilament lines have fluorescent brighteners that make the line much more visible in the air; this increased visibility can be a big help when you're fishing and trying to keep track of your line.

Monofilament line is substantially weakened by nicks or small cuts, and you should check the few feet of line nearest your lure often for such damage. Retie the lure if nec-

essary after trimming off the damaged line. The following story is a good way to remember to check your line.

For reasons known only to these unpredictable fish, Charlie Shaw had been having the best day of life with big muskellunge on a Wisconsin lake. It was mid-October, gray and cold with enough wind to put a chop on the surface—ideal muskie weather. After only two fish in August and September, Charlie had already hooked three that morning and landed one, a 27-pounder (12-kg) that he'd weighed in the net and carefully released.

He anchored off a rocky point and started casting toward shore, jerking the big surface plug back toward him in quick sweeps and hoping to excite a muskie into striking. His second cast had barely landed when the plug disappeared in a wild splash. The muskel-

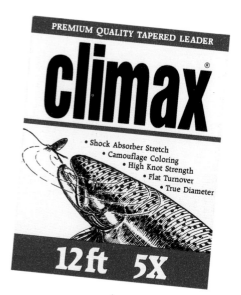

One attribute of fly-fishing leaders is stretch, which means the leader acts as a shock absorber and helps to prevent a fish from breaking the line.

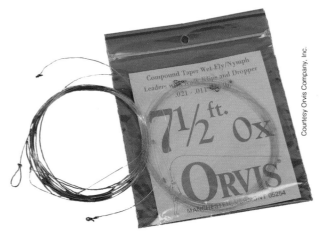

This wet-fly leader features small clips to which your flies can be attached without additional knots.

If you have a choice, use a light-colored floating fly line such as this one to make your casts easier to see in the air and on the water.

lunge came half out of the water, and Shaw could see its wicked teeth surrounding his plug as its great head trashed back and forth. The muskie turned and ran hard for deep water as Charlie strained on the rod.

Suddenly there was nothing. Just a slack, empty line. Charlie reeled up his line and looked sadly at where other fish that morning had frayed his line, damage that had finally let go under the strain of a good fish. It's been ten years, and Charlie is still cursing when I see him, but he does check his line these days.

Fly lines, however, are a different matter. Modern synthetic fly lines were developed in 1952. Although it's still possible to buy a natural silk fly line, the labor costs of hand-braiding the silk make these lines extremely costly. Braided Dacron™ is now used for the level core of most fly lines, over which is a tough, tapered plastic coating. The coating itself usually contains thousands of micro-

scopic hollow spheres, which make the line float. Most fly lines are 30 to 35 yards (27 to 31.5 m) long— about as far as an expert can cast a conventional fly line. Typical fishing distances are usually much less than this.

Fly-line tapers affect your casting and delivery of the fly, and they come in three basic shapes. Level lines are the least expensive

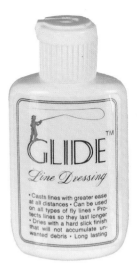

Use a cleaner to free fly lines from dirt, which makes casting difficult. Match fly-fishing leaders (below) to the fly and fish size.

Courtesy Umpqua Feather Merchants

and cast adequately, but their lack of a taper at the front tends to make the fly land hard on the water, which can scare the fish. Double-tapered lines taper down to a fine point at each end, which adds delicacy to the cast. When one end wears out, you can reverse the line on the reel to get a new front taper. Weight-forward tapers are used by most experienced fly anglers because they are the most effective for distance casting—and they also still preserve some delicacy. Weight-forward lines feature a front taper down to a fine point and a short rear taper followed by a thinner running line.

Fly lines are now available that float, sink, or both, allowing flies to be fished on the surface or at any depth down to a practical limit of 30 or 40 feet (9 or 12 m). There are sinking-tip lines in which the first 10 to 30 feet (3 to 9 m) sink and the remainder floats. There are also full-sinking lines for maximum fishing depth. Finally, there are shooting tapers, which are short (about 30 feet [3 m]) fly lines that are usually backed by ultrafine fly line or monofilament to give maximum casting distance. Shooting tapers usually sink, and are most commonly used in steelhead fishing.

A labeling system on fly-line boxes enables you to choose the proper line. The first letter or letters designates the line's taper: L (level), DT (double-taper), WF (weight-forward), or ST (shooting taper). The next number specifies the line weight according to the AFTMA system (page 67) that allows you to match

RAINBOW TROUT

Rainbow trout are native to the Pacific-drainage mountain ranges of western North America, from which they've been distributed to suitable habitat worldwide. They are found in both rivers and lakes, and are a favorite of both commercial and public fish hatcheries, which raise and stock them by the millions across the country every year. Rainbows have reached weights over 50 pounds (22.5 kg), but this large size is most unusual. The most commonly caught rainbows average from less than a pound up to 2 pounds (.45 kg to .9 kg). Anglers' catches will vary widely in size depending upon the river or lake where they are found. Lake rainbows are typically, but not always, larger than river rainbows.

Fishing methods for rainbow trout vary immensely. Fly anglers find that these trout usually rise more readily to a fly than other trout species, so rainbows are a popular dry-fly fish in many streams and rivers. Rainbows tend to cruise the open deep waters of lakes and ponds, unlike brown and brook trout, which often hug the shoreline. This often means that rainbows can best be caught by trolling a small spoon or swimming plug from a boat in mid-lake.

Prime times for fishing rainbow trout are spring and autumn when surface waters are coolest, and the fish are nearest the surface. Hot weather can force the fish to go deep in search of cooler water, and you'll have to fish as deeply as 30 to 50 feet (9 to 15 m) to find fish in midsummer. Rainbows that have been stocked from a hatchery are often caught using corn kernels or bits of marshmallow for bait, but wild, stream-bred fish are rarely caught in this manner, and are sometimes taken on such dry flies as a Royal Wulff or Humpy.

Be sure to check your monofilament spinning line after landing a fish to make sure it hasn't been abraded and weakened near the lure.

the line to your rod. The last letter(s) tell you if the line is a floater (F) or a sinker (S). Thus WF6F is a weight-forward, 6-weight, floating line.

Fly-fishing leaders are used in conjunction with the line to provide a tapered, nearly invisible connection to the fly. These are typically tapered, single-strand (knotless) monofilament leaders that may range from 7½ to 12 feet (2.25 to 3.6 m) long. The thick end is attached to the front of the fly line with a Nail Knot (page 123), and should be about two-thirds of the fly line's diameter at its end. The leader tapers to a fine level point, or tippet,

where the fly is attached. Tippet sizes are given as "X" designations, which derive from an archaic measuring system used when leaders were made from drawn silkworm gut. The smallest is 8X, which is only about .003 inches (.1 mm) in diameter and about one-pound-(.45-kg-) test, and the largest is OX, which usually has a 10- or 12-pound (4.5- or 5.4-kg) breaking strength. The latter is a good bass bug size, while many trout anglers start with a 9-foot (2.7-m), 4X leader for medium-size trout flies. Since tying on and changing flies will eventually reduce the tippet's length, leader-tippet material is also available on

When using wet flies and nymphs in rough water, a sinking-tip fly line will get your fly down to the fish most quickly.

small spools that you can carry to lengthen or change the tippet as necessary.

For fish with very sharp teeth, such as pickerel, northern pike, and muskellunge, spincasters and bait-casters may want to add a wire leader to the end of their line at the lure. These are commonly available in 6- to 24-inch (15- to 60-cm) lengths with a snap at one end, a swivel at the other, and at rated breaking strengths that usually exceed that of your line. Fly anglers can also use these leaders for sharp-toothed fish, but many people have found the addition of a short, monofilament shock tippet at the fly will produce more strikes. This shock leader should be ultra-heavy monofilament, testing at 40 or 60 pounds (18 or 27 kg).

There are a couple of specialty lines you may encounter, both used for deep freshwater trolling for fish such as lake trout in big, deep lakes. These are lead-core and wire trolling lines. Lead-core lines feature a solid strand of lead inside a braided Dacron™ line. Wire lines are simply solid wire. In both cases, the weight and small diameters of these lines will carry a lure extremely deep on a slow troll. Neither line can be used for casting and they usually require large capacity reels.

Chapter 13
Accessories

Finally, we come to the tacklebox itself, where our lures and accessories ideally lead a tangle-free and neat existence until we need them. The tacklebox may be just that—a box—or a series of boxes or, in the case of fly anglers, a multipocketed vest designed to carry everything needed for a day of fishing along the river. The design of the box itself must be considered as well as those few accessory items no angler should be without.

Freshwater tackleboxes are of two basic types. Some boxes feature cantilevered and partitioned trays that open accordion-style when the box's lid is opened. These are handy in that the entire contents is visible at a glance. The second style features partitioned drawers that can be slid open one at a time. This style takes much less room to open and close when in a crowded fishing boat, and I prefer it for that reason. In either case, make sure your box is worm-proof. Plastic worms and other baits contain a compound that literally attacks and dissolves some plastic boxes, and makes an incredible mess. Worm-proof boxes are usually labeled as such, but, if in doubt, make sure to ask your dealer before buying a box. The larger compartments of some boxes have a special rack for spinner-baits and jigs, which is almost essential if you're a bass angler.

I often travel with one or more tackleboxes and after securing the lid tightly with duct tape, I sometimes check the box as airline luggage. Not all airlines permit this; you should check first. In any case, here's a descriptive list of what's in my own box, other than lures, that may help you to assemble the contents of yours.

This tacklebox is ideal for very large lures.

BLACK VINYL TAPE: A small roll of black vinyl tape is good for fixing loose reelseats or making emergency repairs to a line guide.

FLASHLIGHT: This item always reminds me of the two anglers fumbling around in a boat after dark. The conversation invariably includes something like: "I thought you were going to bring it!" The same goes for spare batteries.

HOOK SHARPENER: Most hooks aren't as sharp as they should be, and this includes factory-installed hooks on lures. A small diamond hone is a good way to touch up hook points after catching a few fish or snagging a lure on a rock.

Sliding trays allow you to mix and match tackle.

INSECT REPELLANT: Use a formula with a high percentage of the active ingredient DEET. These solutions can damage many synthetics, including fishing line, rod finishes, and sunglasses, so be careful.

LEAD SINKERS: These again should be appropriate in size and style to whatever fishing you happen to be doing. You might want to carry an assortment of plastic-worm weights from ⅟₁₆ to ½ ounce (1.75 to 14 g) in size.

Courtesy Plano Molding Co. (all photos)

LINE CLIPPERS: These can be simple lever-type fingernail clippers for trimming knots in everything except wire line, which would damage the cutters.

This two-sided box has a secure lid and separate trays.

Polarized sunglasses are essential angling gear.

LONG-NOSED PLIERS: Essential for removing a lure from the mouth of a deeply hooked fish. These are also available with a wire cutter at the back that can be used for trimming wire leaders, but more importantly, can be used for cutting a hook that gets caught on you or anything else. Look for stainless-steel (rust-free) models.

POLARIZED SUNGLASSES: These will prevent headaches from squinting in the sun and protect your eyes at the same time. Polarized glasses cut the water-surface glare, enabling you to spot fish much more easily.

REEL LUBE/PARTS: Most reel makers also supply a lubricant and often a few spare parts, and it pays to carry them with you. The part most likely to fail on any spinning reel is the bail spring. You should order an extra from the maker after you buy your reel.

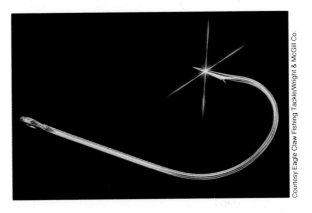

You'll need spare hooks and a hook sharpener, too.

SNAP SWIVELS: A clip for easy lure changing attached to a swivel that can turn freely and help prevent line twist when fishing with a wide variety of lures. These come in several sizes and should be matched to your lure size. Ball-bearing swivels work best, but are more expensive than other types.

SPARE HOOKS: These may be whatever bait-fishing hooks you happen to be using or a supply of plastic-worm hooks. Always have several sizes of each type of hook you use. You may also want to keep some spare treble hooks and split rings on hand to replace damaged hooks on lures.

This box offers easy access to each side separately.

SPARE SPOOLS/LINE: It's easiest to quickly change to an extra spool when the line on your reel becomes badly tangled, or when you want to go to a different size line. At the very least, be sure you've got some extra line.

SUNBLOCK: Fortunately, dangers of overexposure to sunlight are now well known. Anglers who are on the water all day stand the risk of severe burns at the very least, not to mention skin cancer. Carry and use a PABA-type sunblock rated at 15 or higher.

TOOLS: All you really need is a small screwdriver with interchangeable slotted and Phillips heads, and a small adjustable wrench.

WOODEN TOOTHPICKS: For Texas-rigging plastic worms (see page 97).

That's the basic tacklebox list, which will probably grow, depending on the kind of fishing you're doing and your personal preferences. You might want to include a small first-aid kit as well. There are some other things you'll need or want that usually aren't kept in a tacklebox, such as a camera and film. Many people are nervous about taking an expensive camera near water. I keep mine in a waterproof self-locking plastic bag unless I'm actually using it.

You'll also probably want some type of landing net. Make sure yours is suited to the biggest fish you might catch. It seems ludicrous to try and land a 40-pound (18-kg) muskie with a small trout net—as a matter of

Courtesy Orvis Company, Inc.

Make sure your landing net will fit the fish you expect to catch. This is a medium-sized trout model.

fact, it's impossible—but such things have been tried simply because of a lack of foresight. Whatever you do, don't buy or use a gaff. Its big, sharp hook kills or maims fish in the landing process and can just as easily hurt you.

A final note for fly anglers: Be sure your fly boxes will allow files to be carried in them without rusting. Sticking a soggy fly into sheepskin or foam guarantees the hook point will rust and break. Fly boxes with open compartments are best, or at least allow the fly to dry before putting it away.

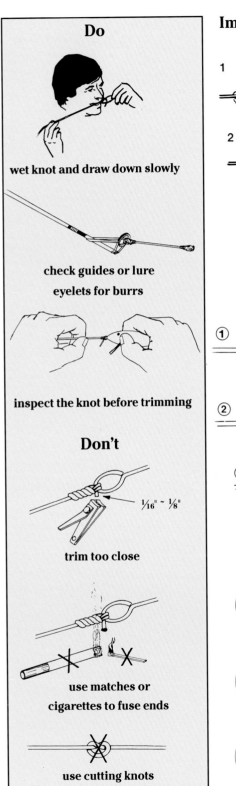

Do

wet knot and draw down slowly

check guides or lure
eyelets for burrs

inspect the knot before trimming

Don't

1/16" ~ 1/8"

trim too close

use matches or
cigarettes to fuse ends

use cutting knots

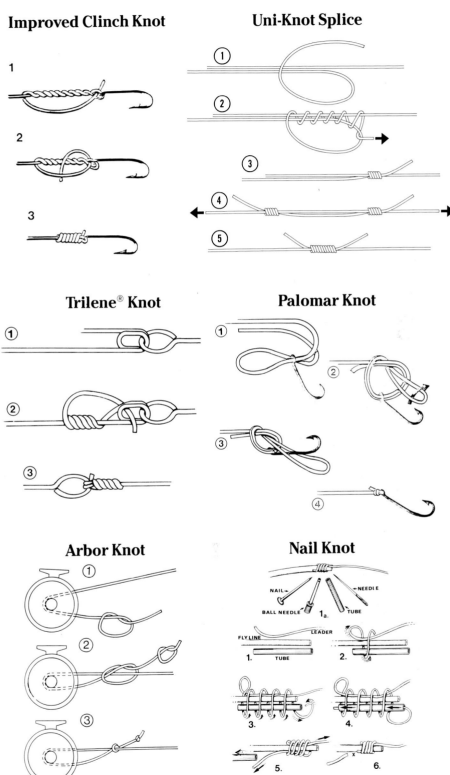

Improved Clinch Knot

1

2

3

Uni-Knot Splice

①
②
③
④
⑤

Trilene® Knot

①
②
③

Palomar Knot

①
②
③
④

Arbor Knot

①
②
③

Nail Knot

NAIL — NEEDLE
BALL NEEDLE — 1a. — TUBE
FLY LINE — LEADER
1. TUBE — 2.
3. — 4.
5. — 6.